Strategic Studies

MW00911297

HIDDEN DRAGON, CROUCHING LION: HOW CHINA'S ADVANCE IN AFRICA IS UNDERESTIMATED AND AFRICA'S POTENTIAL UNDERAPPRECIATED

David E. Brown

September 2012

*****

Comments pertaining to this report are invited and should be forwarded to: Director, Strategic Studies Institute, U.S. Army War College, 47 Ashburn Drive, Carlisle, PA 17013-5010.

*****

*****

ISBN 1-58487-542-9

FOREWORD

The Strategic Studies Institute (SSI) has maintained close and positive professional ties with our colleagues at the Africa Center for Strategic Studies (ACSS) in Washington, DC, since ACSS's founding in 1999. The Africa Center is the preeminent U.S. Department of Defense (DoD) institution for strategic security studies, research, and outreach in Africa. I am pleased that SSI and ACSS are once more able to collaborate in the publication of this monograph, entitled *Hidden Dragon, Crouching Lion: How China's Advance in Africa is Underestimated and Africa's Potential Underappreciated.* Its author, David E. Brown, is currently the Senior Diplomatic Advisor at ACSS. He brings unique perspectives to the important foreign policy issue of China's rapid commercial and political advance in Africa, having served eight times in China and Africa as a Foreign Service Officer at U.S. Embassies, U.S. Consulates, and the American Institute in Taiwan.

This monograph is part of our Advancing Strategic Thought Series precisely because its topic is so important. As Mr. Brown stresses, the explosive growth of China's economic interests in Africa is arguably the most important trend in the continent's foreign relations since the end of the Cold War. China-Africa trade passed the $1 billion mark in 1990, jumped to $10 billion in 2000, and accelerated again, increasing 15-fold in a little over a decade to $150 billion in 2011. China's rapidly expanding ties with Africa catapulted China past the United States in 2010 as Africa's top trading partner. Mr. Brown predicts that by 2020, China's projected expansion of trade, investment, and development assistance is likely to secure economic and political influence for Beijing in Africa that at least rivals, if not surpasses, that enjoyed by Europe and the United States over the last 150 years.

Moreover, as the monograph emphasizes, China's quest to build a strategic partnership with Africa must also be seen in the broader context of the central strategic objective of Beijing's foreign policy: promoting the peaceful rise of the People's Republic of China (PRC) as a global superpower. What China is now consolidating in Africa is just one part of a broader network of global alliances that support not only Beijing's putative leadership in the developing world, but its emerging role as a global power rivaling the United States. A cornerstone of China's strategy is also the recognition that its national security ultimately depends on a strong, internationally competitive economy. With this in mind, China increasingly turns to Africa not only for resources to fuel its development, but also for markets to sustain its growing economy and ultimately support its longer-term aspirations to surpass the United States as the world's preeminent power.

An important but secondary theme of this monograph is that Africa has become an attractive trading partner for China not only for its natural resources, but as a growing market. Africa's rapid growth since 2000 has occurred not just because of higher commodity prices, but, more importantly, because of other factors, including improved political governance, macroeconomic stability, microeconomic reforms, increased globalization, urbanization, an expanding labor force, and a rising middle class. Mr. Brown argues that China has been at least 10 years ahead of American firms in strategic perceptions and thinking about Africa's economic promise. While many in the West remain Afro-pessimists, he says, the Chinese have been guarded Afro-optimists or, perhaps more accurately,

Afro-realists who recognize both the continent's great promise and significant risk.

SSI is pleased to offer this monograph in fulfillment of its mission to assist U.S. Army and DoD senior leaders and strategic thinkers in understanding the key issues of the day.

DOUGLAS C. LOVELACE, JR.
Director
Strategic Studies Institute

ABOUT THE AUTHOR

DAVID E. BROWN is a career member of the Senior Foreign Service, who joined the Africa Center for Strategic Studies (ACSS) as Senior Diplomatic Advisor in August 2011. His prior Africa experience includes serving as the Senior Advisor to the J-5 (Strategy, Plans, and Programs) Director of the U.S. Africa Command (AFRICOM) in Stuttgart, Germany; three times as Deputy Chief of Mission at U.S. Embassies in Cotonou, Benin; Nouakchott, Mauritania; and Ouagadougou, Burkina Faso; and as Economic Officer at the U.S. Consulate-General in Lubumbashi, Democratic Republic of the Congo. Mr. Brown's non-Africa overseas tours have been as Consul General in Chengdu, China, and Economic Officer in Beijing; Tokyo, Japan; and Moscow, Russia. He has also served in Washington, DC, as the Director of the Office of Environmental Policy; as Economic Officer in the Bureau of Economic, Energy, and Business Affairs (EEB) responsible for trade policy with developing countries, including Africa; and on the Canada desk, with responsibilities for economic, consular, and law enforcement issues. Prior to joining the U.S. Department of State, he worked in Miami as the business manager of the Latin American Bureau of CBS News. Mr. Brown holds a B.A. in government (political science) from Cornell University; an MBA from the University of Chicago, specializing in finance; and an MBA from the University of Louvain, Belgium, with majors in econometrics and international business.

INTRODUCTION

The first part of the title of this monograph is arguably a misnomer. How can China — the Dragon — be hidden, if its presence in Africa is so obvious to Africans? Africans see evidence of the new China everywhere, from Chinese traders who have appeared in their markets, to Chinese construction or mining firms, and to even the Chinese consumer products found everywhere. Yet, for most Americans, China in Africa is a hidden dragon. They remain unaware that a rising China — the greatest partner and rival of the United States in the 21st century — has already arrived in a big way on a continent that is the ancestral home of so many Americans as well as the cradle of all mankind. Americans also remain stuck in old images of Africa: famine, poverty, and desperation, instead of the continent's new reality of progress, prosperity, and hope.

Two members of the Africa Center for Strategic Studies in Washington, DC, recently exchanged e-mails about China, Africa, and the West. The first, based in the Center's regional office in Addis Ababa, Ethiopia, recounted news that Chinese President Hu Jintao would visit the Ethiopian capital in January 2012 to inaugurate a new $200 million headquarters of the African Union paid for by Beijing — China's greatest ever gift to Africa and a soft power *tour de force*. The second colleague's response to this e-mail was brief, but wise: "China rises . . . while the West sleeps." China is indeed rising, and the extraordinary increase over the last 20 years in the breadth, depth, and complexity of its economic interests and presence in Africa mirrors its rise in other parts of the world.

This monograph is divided into four parts: Part 1 describes how China is leading other developing countries — including the other three "BRIC" countries (Brazil, Russia, and India) — in expanding aid, trade, and investment with Africa, defined here as North and Sub-Saharan Africa. Part 2 answers five major questions regarding the China-Africa economic relationship: Why China chose to expand its economic ties to Africa; why it has been so successful in expanding rapidly; whether new trade credits and development loans are creating a new African debt burden; whether African industrialization will be aided or hindered by China; and what the impact of new, nonstate Chinese actors (companies and individuals) will be on Africa. Part 3 addresses the strategic importance to China of its oil, minerals, and agriculture trade with and investments in Africa, while Part 4 discusses U.S. responses to China's advance into Africa.

HIDDEN DRAGON, CROUCHING LION: HOW CHINA'S ADVANCE IN AFRICA IS UNDERESTIMATED AND AFRICA'S POTENTIAL UNDERAPPRECIATED

SUMMARY

The explosive growth of China's economic interests in Africa is arguably the most important trend in the continent's foreign relations arena since the end of the Cold War. China-Africa trade passed the $1 billion mark in 1990, jumped to $10 billion in 2000, and accelerated again, increasing 15-fold in a little over a decade to $150 billion in 2011. China's rapidly expanding ties with Africa catapulted China past the United States in 2010 as Africa's top trading partner. China's projected expansion of trade, investment, and development assistance is likely by 2020 to secure economic and political influence for Beijing in Africa that at least rivals, if not surpasses, that enjoyed by Europe and the United States over the last 150 years.

China's advance in Africa is 10 years ahead of similar moves by the other BRIC (Brazil, Russia, and India) emerging market leaders. Other developing countries in the Middle East and Asia are also entering African markets. With the important exception of the petroleum sector, China already has largely displaced traditional colonial powers and the United States as the predominant economic power in Africa. This displacement also mirrors Beijing's ongoing rapid expansion in Latin America and exemplifies China's rise in the early-21st century as a second great power rivaling the United States.

China's four main interests in Africa are: securing natural resources, including petroleum and strategic minerals; tapping an emerging market that has great long-term potential and is underestimated by the West; securing political support from African nations in the United Nations (UN); and ensuring Taiwan's diplomatic isolation. The first two economic interests now dominate the latter two political interests — a role reversal from the Maoist and immediate post-Maoist periods ending in 1978 — and reflect Beijing's recognition that national security ultimately comes from economic strength.

Africa has become an attractive trading partner for China, not only for its natural resources, but as a growing market. Africa's rapid growth since 2000 — averaging 4.5 percent annually — has been due in part to a commodities "super cycle,"[1] but more importantly to other factors, including improved political governance, macroeconomic stability, microeconomic reforms, increased globalization, urbanization, an expanding labor force, and a rising middle class.

The key milestones influencing the recent history of China's relations with Africa are: 1978, when Beijing's "reform and opening" policies started; 1993, when China became an oil-importing country; 1995, when China's State Council ordered that aid, trade credits, and development finance to Africa be tied to Chinese commercial interests; 2000, when China started its triennial Heads of State summitry with Africa; and 2001, when China joined the World Trade Organization (WTO) and also launched its "going-out" policy to support the development of Chinese multinational firms, including those in Africa.

China's rapid and successful expansion in Africa is due to a multiplicity of factors, including economic diplomacy that is clearly superior to that of the United States, which cut back on support for U.S. business in

Africa just as China surged ahead. Beijing skillfully supports its economic diplomacy in Africa through triennial heads of state summits; sustained high-level bilateral visits; a universal diplomatic presence in Africa (except for four small countries where Taipei makes its last stand)[2]; symbolic diplomacy exemplified by the new Chinese-built African Union headquarters opened in Addis Ababa, Ethiopia, in January 2012; bilateral trade, investment, and tax agreements; and vastly expanded "soft power" diplomacy — cultural centers, a volunteer corps, and international visitor programs — lifted from the U.S. diplomatic playbook. Another factor in China's success has been its aggressive, integrated, and mercantilist policies for official aid, preferential trade credits, and development finance — all of which draw upon China's own development experience and an Asian-style, state-led growth model.

China, aided by its mercantilist policy of undervaluing its currency, has been successful in the Africa market because of the lower cost of its goods and services, but is also moving up the value-added chain for goods and becoming more competitive in services, especially engineering and construction. China has hurt African industrialization in textiles, negating the positive effects of the Africa Growth and Opportunity Act (AGAO) after the phaseout of the WTO Multifiber Agreement in 2005. At the same time, China has aided nontextile industrialization by: 1) restructuring its industry to "sunset" to Africa some of its low-tech, labor-intensive, and/or environmentally problematic industries such as shoes and leather; 2) adding backward and forward integration to its mining investments, and upstream goods used in construction; and, 3) supporting infrastructure improvements, including those in new Special Economic Zones (SEZs) now under construction.

Western donors are concerned that China's "no strings attached" approach to development risks undoing decades of Western efforts to promote good governance, revenue transparency, and responsible natural resource development in Africa; corrupts African elites; unfairly promotes China's interests at the expense of other non-African nations by violating Organization for Economic Cooperation and Development (OECD) norms for aid and trade credits; free-rides on Highly Indebted Poor Country (HIPC) debt relief; and risks new unsustainable debts for African nations. China denies these charges, arguing that the commodity offtake agreements that are part of some new loans mitigate risk for China and ensure that African countries use resource revenues in ways that invest in development instead of being squandered by elites. Beijing is filling an important gap in Western aid—and doing well commercially—by focusing on improving Africa's infrastructure.

While China's engagement with Africa has up to now been primarily led by the Chinese government- and state-owned enterprises, nonstate actors, including privatized Chinese corporations and citizens, are increasingly important. These nonstate actors are making a contribution to the diversity and depth of Chinese trade and investment with Africa, but are also aggravating a host of problems, including rampant corruption, the flouting of labor and environmental laws, and the sale of counterfeit goods. Large-scale immigration by Chinese to Africa—by some estimates, totaling over 1 million people—is creating tensions, particularly with African retail traders. Some African politicians and the continent's civil society are starting to debate the costs and benefits of China's growing economic ties with the continent.

China, more than the United States, needs Africa as a source of oil to fuel its rapid industrialization and diversify supplies away from the volatile Middle East. One-third of China's oil imports come from the continent, versus 18-19 percent for the United States. China's "oil diplomacy" has been most successful in Angola (due to corruption and financing deals linked to infrastructure needs) and in other African countries with smaller fields — ignored as marginal or politically sensitive by major Western companies. China's use of rare-earth metals to threaten Japan over a territorial issue and the United States over Taiwan arms sales suggests that the United States should carefully monitor China's mining investments in strategic defense-critical minerals in southern Africa. The U.S. Department of Defense (DoD) may ultimately choose to replenish stockpiles sold off after the end of the Cold War. Food security is a major issue for China, but Africa is not seen as an important source of future food imports. While Africa has 60 percent of the world's total uncultivated arable land, the Chinese have not been large-scale buyers or lessees of African land, in part because Beijing fears being accused of a land grab.

The official U.S. rhetoric is that China's rise in Africa should not be seen as a zero-sum game with the West, but areas for real U.S.-China cooperation to help Africa will remain elusive. The fundamental problem is China's domestic politics, in which many actors benefit from China's current modus operandi in Africa and, in any event, are hyper-mistrustful of the United States. The United States could help itself, however, by improving its economic diplomacy and statecraft, including, initiating a presidential summit with African heads of state; better funding of U.S. Government agencies providing trade advocacy, export credits, and investment insurance; and reforming the U.S. Foreign Commercial Service and how U.S. diplomats are trained and rewarded for commercial advocacy. The United States should also adequately fund its own soft power efforts, focusing on public diplomacy. U.S. policymakers should also continue to seek areas where cooperation with China regarding Africa may be possible. In light of African-led efforts in the UN, one area worth exploring is cooperation with Beijing to improve maritime security in the Gulf of Guinea by training and equipping West and Central African navies and coast guards.

PART I

CHINA LEADS THE DEVELOPING WORLD IN FOSTERING ECONOMIC TIES TO AFRICA

THE HIDDEN DRAGON: CHINA'S MAIN INTERESTS IN AFRICA AND PLACE IN THE WORLD

The People's Republic of China (PRC), founded in 1949, started providing aid to African nations in the early 1950s, first to Egypt. China's supreme leader, Mao Zedong, aided Africa's newly independent nations in the late 1950s and early 1960s, in competition with Moscow and Washington. After a period of retrenchment in the 1970s, China's involvement in Africa, both diplomatic and commercial, came alive again in the 1980s as an international extension of Deng Xiaoping's policies of "reform and opening," which were initiated in 1978. China-Africa economic ties gained further momentum in the early 1990s, due most importantly to China's search for natural resources. Today, 20 years later, China has the same four core interests in Africa, albeit with a shift in priorities:

1. *Securing Natural Resources*: China's number one interest in Africa is to increase access to energy, minerals, and raw materials to fuel China's rapid industrialization and emerging consumer society. China's National Oil Companies (NOCs) are developing oil fields in Africa, and hope one day to compete as technological equals with Western companies. Chinese firms are already working hyperactively in African mines, from Guinea's bauxite to Niger's uranium to Zambia's copper.[3]

7

2. *Tapping an Emerging Market*: For China, Africa is a growing, one billion-person market, with increasing disposable income and an expanding middle class. Africa's collective gross domestic product (GDP) will grow by $1 trillion by 2020, taking it to a total of $2.6 trillion.[4] Investment in Africa can also potentially facilitate Beijing's efforts to restructure China's own economy away from low-cost, labor-intensive, and/or heavily polluting industries.

3. *United Nation Votes*: African countries account for more than one-quarter of UN member-states and votes. By cultivating African nations, China seeks to win their support in international forums and secure its status as a rising power. For example, when the neuralgic issue of Tibet became an issue in 2008 in the UN Human Rights Council, China leaned on African nations to remain silent or even make supportive statements.[5]

4. *Isolating Taiwan*: The PRC seeks to end Taipei's official diplomatic presence in Africa and replace it with recognition of Beijing. Some observers believe that since Taiwan's election in 2008 of President Ma Yingjiu (who was re-elected in January 2012), there has been an informal truce between Beijing and Taipei concerning competition for diplomatic recognition.[6] Others argue, however, that the countries worldwide that still recognize Taipei are so few in number (23), and that the contest is essentially over.

While China's interests in Africa until the end of the Mao era in 1976 were mainly political, they are now predominantly economic, with 1) and 2) replacing the current 3) and 4) as China's top priorities.

AFRICA: AIDING CHINA'S PEACEFUL RISE AS A SUPERPOWER

China's quest to build a strategic partnership with Africa must also be seen in the broader context of the central strategic objective of Beijing's foreign policy: promoting the PRC's peaceful rise as a global super-power.[7] What China is now consolidating in Africa is just one part of a broader network of global alliances that support not only Beijing's putative leadership in the developing world, but also its emerging role as a global power rivaling the United States. A corner-stone of China's strategy is also the recognition that its national security ultimately depends on a strong, internationally competitive economy. With this in mind, China increasingly turns to Africa not only for resources to fuel its development, but also for markets to sustain its growing economy and ultimately sup-port its longer-term aspirations to surpass the United States as the world's preeminent power. Many of the trends described in this monograph are also clearly visible in Latin America, a traditional zone of influ-ence of the United States and a relatively new region for China.

The tactics that China is using in Africa to realize its strategic ambitions include: offering powerful eco-nomic incentives in the form of vastly expanded trade, investment, and development assistance; expanded soft power diplomatic instruments; and peacekeep-ing and military cooperation (currently limited, but expanding, e.g., through Chinese offers to support the African Union Mission in Somalia (AMISOM) and the December 2011 talks with the Seychelles to establish a resupply facility, ostensibly to fight piracy). Beijing also tries to distinguish its relations with Africa from those of Western powers by framing relations in terms of Third World solidarity, of its historical ties to Africa starting under Mao, and of calls for expanded ties based on "mutual respect," "noninterference in internal affairs," and "win-win" outcomes.[8]

Some observers say that Beijing's moves have been so rapid, momentous, and successful that they have already put China on par with long-established Western powers regarding Africa. China-Africa trade passed the $1 billion level in 1980, jumped to $10 billion in 2000,[9] and again increased 15-fold in a little more than a decade to $150 billion in 2011. China's projected rapid expansion of trade, investment, and development assistance is likely in the second decade of the 21st century to succeed in securing economic and political ties to African nations that at least rival, if not surpass, the relations and influence that European nations and the United States have enjoyed in Africa over the last 150 years.[10]

OTHER BRICS AND THE DEVELOPING WORLD ALSO INTERESTED IN AFRICA

While China's increased presence in Africa is the single most important foreign policy development for the continent since the end of the Cold War, it is also an important component of two broader megatrends in Africa in the new millennium. It is not possible to compare China's expanding presence in Africa with that of the West without also appreciating these broader trends:

1. Increased involvement in Africa by BRICs other than China, i.e., the emerging powers of Brazil, India, and Russia. The BRICs' combined foreign direct investment (FDI) in Africa has already surpassed the

U.S. total for the continent. Growing interest in African resource investments by other BRICs has granted African commodity exporters a stronger hand in bargaining with the Chinese. In May 2011, India's Prime Minister announced $5 billion in credits for African governments over the next 3 years—a move widely seen as an attempt by New Delhi to present itself as a rival partner to China in Africa.[11]

2. Expansion in Africa's South-South trade with the developing world is eclipsing traditional North-South trade with the European Union (EU), the United States, and Japan. The International Monetary Fund (IMF) reports that for Sub-Saharan Africa (and for North Africa as well), there has been a significant and rapid reorientation of exports toward China, India, and other developing countries over the past decade. More than half of the region's trade (both exports and imports) is now with nontraditional partners, and investment flows are moving along a similar course. Between 1990 and 2010, the share of Sub-Saharan Africa's exports to advanced economies declined from 78 percent to 52 percent, and the share of Sub-Saharan Africa's imports from those countries declined from 73 percent to 43 percent. Most of this reorientation has occurred during the past 10 years. By 2010, the share of Sub-Saharan Africa trade with China, India, and Brazil reached approximately 17 percent, 6 percent, and 3 percent, respectively, rising from negligible shares in 1990. Very importantly, this reorientation has largely occurred through trade creation rather than trade diversion, as engagement with traditional Western partners has continued to grow in recent years, though at a much slower pace than that with new partners.[12] This trend was accelerated by the global financial crisis starting in 2008, which hit developed countries harder

than emerging economies. As World Bank President Robert Zoellick said in September 2010: "China's South-South partnership with Africa in trade, investment, and exchange of know-how can become an important source of growth in the post-crisis era."[13]

Africa's key South-South partners other than China are:

- *India.* This country is a distant second behind China in terms of its expanding engagement on the continent, but is striving to catch up. This new Sino-Indo scramble for Africa also reflects a broader, more intense global competition between these two emerging Asian powers. China's trade with Africa in 2010 totaled $126.9 billion, or two-and-a-half times India's $51 billion. At the same time, India's trade with Africa in 2010 had increased more than 50-fold (from $967 million in 1990),[14] and is expected to rise to $70 billion by 2015.[15] China has almost twice as many embassies in Africa as India, and its investment, loans, and aid flows to Africa are much higher.[16] Recognizing China's lead in Africa, India has stepped up its efforts to gain an economic foothold on the continent. New Delhi sponsored the second India-Africa Summit in Addis Ababa in May 2011. At least in its early stages, the competition between Beijing and New Delhi focuses most importantly on Africa's natural resources. India's state Oil and Natural Gas Corporation (ONGC) signed an agreement for joint exploration and refining projects with Angola, which is seen as a precursor to future rounds of licensing in which ONGC hopes to win oil blocks. Toward this end, India has already offered to invest billions in building and refurbishing refineries in Angola. Beijing, however, has a huge head start. China has already granted Luanda an estimated $10 billion in loans, compared to only $70 million in Indian loans, and has a larger physical presence in Angola — with than 40,000 workers compared to India's 1,500.[17]

- *Brazil.* Although well behind China and India, Brazil has made its presence felt throughout much of Africa, and not just in Portuguese-speaking countries. The sharply upward-growth trajectory of Brazil's trade with Africa has been similar to that of China and India, with the trade of $3.1 billion in 2000 leaping to $27.6 billion in 2011.[18] From 2003 to 2010, Brazilian President Lula da Silva made 11 trips to 25 African nations and doubled the number of Brazilian embassies in Africa.[19] Current Brazilian President Dilma Rousseff announced in April 2012 the plan of her government to establish a special fund for Africa to finance development projects together with the African Development Bank (ADB) and World Bank. During the same month, the private Brazilian bank, BTG Pactual, announced the launch of a $1 billion fund for investment in Africa.[20]

- *Russia.* Meanwhile, Russia is attempting a comeback in Africa. It had retreated from the continent after the breakup of the Soviet Union, closing nine embassies in Sub-Saharan Africa in 1992. Russian President Dmitry Medvedev traveled in 2009 to Egypt, Nigeria, Angola, and Namibia to shore up Russian energy, mining, and telecommunication deals.[21] However,

Russia's trade with Africa was a distant fourth behind China, India, and Brazil, reaching $3.5 billion in 2009.[22] Russia organized a meeting in December 2011 in Addis Ababa, Ethiopia, with 250 African businessmen along with Russian representatives of Gasprombank, Lukoil, and the Russian Railroad Company interested in gas and oil exploration and railroad development.[23]

- *Non-BRICS Developing Countries.* There are also growing trade and investment flows into Africa from the Middle East and elsewhere in Asia. Turkey stepped up its engagement in Africa beginning in 2005, and is an important player in North Africa and the Horn of Africa. Iran has focused its attention on northeastern Africa, but is expanding its relations throughout the continent in part as an effort to escape political and economic isolation. Government ministers from 35 African countries attended the third biennial Korea-Africa Economic Cooperation Ministerial Conference in 2010.[24] Other emerging countries that are either re-engaging in Africa or arriving for the first time include Saudi Arabia, the United Arab Emirates, Malaysia, Thailand, Singapore, Indonesia, and Vietnam.[25] Reflecting this shift, Asia's share of African trade doubled from 1990 through 2008 to 28 percent, while Western Europe's portion shrank from 51 percent to 28 percent.[26]

TEN YEARS OF SUCCESSFUL AFRICA-CHINA TRADE: THE DRAGON FLIES MORE SWIFTLY THAN THE EAGLE

If a June 2010 report by the McKinsey Global Institute is an accurate reflection of renewed U.S. business interest in Africa, then China has been at least 10 years ahead of American firms in strategic perceptions and thinking about Africa's economic promise. While many in the West remain Afro-pessimists, the Chinese have been guarded Afro-optimists or, perhaps more accurately, Afro-realists who recognize both the continent's great promise and significant risk.

China's confidence in Africa is paying dividends. While Chinese trade (exports and imports) with the world rose eightfold from 2000 to 2010, it rose more than 11-fold with Africa during this same period[27] (and 15-fold from 2000 to 2011).[28] China, Africa's largest trading partner, accounted for 10.4 percent of the continent's total trade in 2010 (up from about 4 percent in 2000), while Africa accounted for about 4 percent of China's global trade — up from about 2 percent in 2000.[29] By comparison, the United States, which was dethroned by China as Africa's top trading partner in 2010, had $113 billion in trade in Africa that year, a 3-fold increase from the $39 billion in trade with Africa in 2000.[30]

China's top trade partners in Africa in 2010 (see Figure 1) were mainly countries indicated with an asterisk in Figure 1, from which it purchases oil and minerals (in $ billions)[31]:

1. South Africa ($25.7)*	11. Kenya ($1.8)
2. Angola ($24.8)*	12. Tanzania ($1.7)
3. Nigeria ($7.8)*	13. Ethiopia ($1.5)
4. Egypt ($7.0)	14. Mauritania ($1.3)*
5. Libya ($6.6)*	15. Gabon ($1.2)*
6. Algeria ($5.2)*	16. Tunisia ($1.1)
7. Congo ($3.5)*	17. Equatorial Guinea ($1.1)*
8. Morocco ($2.9)	18. Cameroon ($1.0)*
9. Zambia ($2.9)*	19. Chad ($0.8)*
10. Ghana ($2.1)	20. Botswana ($.04)*

*Indicates country from which China purchased oil and minerals.

Figure 1. China's Top Trade Partners in Africa in 2010 (in $ billions).

China's strong exports to Africa also reflect its increased global competitiveness in a broader range of products. In 2000, China's exports to Africa consisted largely of textiles and clothing (28 percent), machinery and transportation equipment (27 percent), and other manufactured goods (26 percent). By 2009, however, Chinese exports to Africa had shifted to high-end capital goods, especially communications equipment (20 percent), road-transport vehicles (19 percent), and electronic machinery (18 percent). Put differently, electro-mechanical products such as machinery, automobiles, and electronics accounted for almost 60 percent of China's exports to Africa—a dramatic increase since 2000.

By contrast, 90 percent of Africa's exports to China in 2010 were oil, minerals, base metals, stone products, and raw logs.[32] About 80 percent of Africa's exports to China come from only five oil- and mineral-exporting nations. Primary products such as cotton and phosphate were formerly the main products exported by Africa to China. In recent years, however, Africa's finished industrial products, such as steel and copper materials, chemical fertilizers, and electronic products, have started to enter the Chinese market. Meanwhile, Africa's exports of farm produce to China have also increased rapidly, albeit from a low base.[33] (See the section on agriculture below.)

Similar to unilateral trade preferences granted by the United States and the EU to Africa, China gives zero-tariff preferences to certain goods exported to China from selected African countries. By July 2010, the number of commodities entitled to the preferential policy increased to more than 4,700 tariff lines,[34] and in the future will include up to 95 percent of the commodities listed in China's customs database. Africa's exports of commodities entitled to preferences have increased rapidly, but still represent only a small fraction of its total imports: in 2009, China imported only $4.5 billion of such products from Africa, including farm produce, leather, stone materials, textiles and garments, machinery parts, base metals, and wood products.[35]

CHINA'S FOREIGN DIRECT INVESTMENT IN AFRICA—LARGE, BUT ESTIMATES DIFFER

Chinese FDI in Africa quadrupled between 2005 and 2009, reaching a cumulative stock of $9.3 billion, according to the PRC Minister of Commerce figures. Renaissance Capital predicts this could soar to $40 billion by 2015 (based on a conservative estimate of $5 billion in annual Chinese FDI).[36] China's investments in Africa at the end of 2009 were increasingly diversified, falling in the following sectors: mining/industry (29.2 percent); manufacturing (22.0 percent); construction (15.8 percent); finance (13.9 percent); business services (5.4 percent); wholesale/retail trade (4.0 percent); scientific research, technical services, and geological prospecting (3.2 percent); farming, forestry, fishing, and animal husbandry (3.1 percent); and others (3.4 percent).[37] The IMF estimated in October 2011 that China accounted for 16 percent of FDI flows to Sub-Saharan Africa, up exponentially from less than 1 percent as recently as 2003.[38]

Chinese official figures for FDI in Africa for the period 2007-10 show an average increase of about $1.5 billion per year if one discounts the exceptional year of 2008, when Industrial and Commercial Bank of China (ICBC) purchased 20 percent of South Africa's Standard Bank for $5.5 billion. In the year 2010, FDI was reported to be $2.1 billion.[39] The Bank of China reported that China's cumulative FDI in Africa was over $10 billion by the end of 2010, about 20 times that in 2003. This being said, there is considerable confusion surrounding this figure and China's definition of direct investment. Some official Chinese figures for investment totals in Africa likely understate the real amount. Even PRC sources cannot agree on the amount of China's FDI that has gone into Africa. For example, the official Xinhua News Agency reported that, by the end of 2010, China had invested about $40 billion in more than 2,000 enterprises in 50 African countries—a figure roughly 400 percent at variance with that of the Bank of China.

While the correct total FDI figure is probably closer to $40 billion than to $10 billion, Western countries collectively have invested much more in Africa, primarily because they started earlier. By the end of 2008, for example, the United States had invested a cumulative total of $37 billion in Sub-Saharan Africa. It is possible that today China is investing more in Africa than any other single country. The primary recipients of Chinese FDI in Africa have been South Africa, Nigeria, Zambia, Sudan, Algeria, and Egypt—all major oil or mineral exporters except Egypt.[40] (The IMF also lists Niger, the Democratic Republic of the Congo [DRC], and Ethiopia as major recipients of Chinese FDI; the first two are major mineral exporters.[41]) Data from the Heritage Foundation suggest that China was responsible for nearly all FDI into the DRC over the period 2005 to 2009, nearly 50 percent into Nigeria, and 20 percent into South Africa.[42] Part of the reason for the wide discrepancies in FDI statistics is that Chinese investments are often channeled through off-shore entities registered in places such as Hong Kong, the Cayman Islands, and others.[43] Hong Kong FDI into Africa was estimated at $5.3 billion in 2008, which helps explain part of the discrepancy.

China's strategic investments in South Africa's financial sector merit particular mention. First, Chinese banks in South Africa are serving their Chinese customers, for whom South Africa has grown into a regional hub where Chinese investors can venture further into the continent.[44] South Africa accounts for fully one-quarter of Chinese FDI in Africa. Second, Chinese banks are taking equity stakes in South African banks in part to gain market intelligence and business in other African countries. For example, ICBC's investment will allow it access to Standard Bank's activities in more than 17 countries. A substantial increase in financing for African infrastructure projects was expected as a result of this investment. This has become evident as an increasing number of joint projects between ICBC and Standard Bank are announced, recently including financing of $825 million for a coal-fired power station in Botswana.[45] The China Development Bank also paid $3 billion for a 3.1 percent stake in Barclays, which has a strong presence in Africa.[46]

PART II:

MAJOR QUESTIONS IN THE CHINA-AFRICA ECONOMIC RELATIONSHIP

As noted above, the rapid expansion of China's economic interests in Africa is arguably the most important trend in the continent's foreign relations arena since the end of the Cold War. To illuminate this trend, this section addresses several key questions about the nature of the China-Africa economic relationship:

1. Why did China choose to expand its economic ties to Africa?

2. Why has China been so successful in expanding these ties?

3. Are China's trade credits and development loans creating a new debt burden for Africa?

4. Will Africa be able to industrialize in part because of, or despite, China?

5. What are the impacts on new nonstate Chinese actors on Africa?

WHY DID CHINA CHOOSE TO EXPAND ITS ECONOMIC TIES TO AFRICA?

The first major question addressed is: "Why did China choose to expand its economic ties to Africa? " Broadly speaking, there are two reasons:

1. The *"pull'* of Africa as an increasingly attractive trade and investment destination, initially as an indispensable supplier of natural resources, but increasingly as an attractive export market and investment target; and,

2. The *"push"* of domestic factors within China itself, including the burgeoning demand for inputs to

feed rapidly rising industrial production, and China's 2001 accession to the WTO. Along with Beijing's mercantilist economic policies, these factors laid the groundwork for China's huge trade surpluses, emerging multinationals, and massive capital reserves.

The Pull of Africa: Turning a Corner toward Sustainable Growth.

Not Just Riding the Latest Commodities Boom. As to Africa's "pull" or attractiveness to China, let us first admit that the beauty of Africa as a trade and investment partner lies in the eye of the beholder. Optimists rightly see the continent as the last emerging market frontier—a risky, but extraordinary, opportunity. They recognize that Africa will continue to take one step backward, but then two forward. These optimists recognize that long gone is the continent's dystopian, gloom-and-doom, "Out of Africa" era of the 1990s during which foreign investors fled.[47]

The Chinese government recognized earlier than others that Africa had made a fundamental shift. By the late 1990s, Beijing officials began to believe that the macroeconomic situation in Africa was taking a favorable turn: the increasing momentum of Africa's economic reform programs was resulting in greater opportunities for Chinese commerce.[48] With 20/20 hindsight, China's early conversion to a believer may have also reflected lessons learned from the success of Beijing's own reform and opening policies, thus providing the Chinese with confidence that Africa's own efforts at economic reform would eventually pay off.

There are still naysayers about Africa's future, of course, but they are fewer than in the past. These naysayers dismiss Africa's recent economic success as primarily the result of an extended supercycle of high commodity prices, and predict a regression to Africa's historical economic underperformance once prices fall. In the view of these pessimists, Africa, the home of one-third of the world's resource-dependent economies, has been mired in a high degree of corruption and dependence on resource rent from which it has yet to escape. They still consider Africa as a target for aid, rather than trade and investment. Consequently, they still view Africa more as a social responsibility investment, rather than a real opportunity for yield.[49]

While this point about the cost of corruption is partly valid, most of the statistical evidence supports the optimists' view that relative progress has been made and that the importance of high commodity prices has been overstated. It is undeniably true that soaring prices for oil, minerals, and other commodities have helped lift Africa's GDP since 2000. However, the McKinsey Global Institute estimated in 2010 that natural resources directly accounted for just 24 percent of the continent's GDP growth from 2000 through 2008. By another estimate, natural resources—and the related government spending they financed—generated just 32 percent of Africa's GDP growth from 2000 through 2008, with the remaining two-thirds-plus coming from other sectors.

From 2000 to 2010, Africa's real GDP grew by 4.7 percent a year, on average—twice the pace of its growth in the 1980s and 1990s. By 2009, Africa's collective GDP of $1.6 trillion was roughly equal to Brazil's or Russia's. Today, the continent remains among the world's fastest-expanding economic regions. In fact, Africa and Asia (excluding Japan) were the only continents that grew during the recent global recession that started in 2008.[50] Though GDP growth in Sub-Saharan

Africa slowed to 2.8 percent in 2009 after averaging 6.6 percent from 2004 to 2008, it bounced back to 5.3 percent in 2010.[51] In 2011, GDP growth rose to 5.1 percent and will be 5.4 percent in 2012 and 5.3 percent in 2013, the IMF predicted.[52] GDP growth is expected to average 5 percent through 2015.[53]

Moreover, Africa's economic growth since 2000 has been widespread, with 27 of its 30 largest economies expanding rapidly. Indeed, countries with and without significant resource exports had similar GDP growth rates. All sectors within African economies also contributed to growth, including natural resources, finance, retail, agriculture, transportation, and telecommunications.

Drivers of Growth within Africa. We will likely never know the thought processes that transpired in 1995 in Chinese ministries, think tanks, and even Zhongnanhai — the residences and offices of China's top leadership — in reformulating China's foreign policy toward Africa during that pivotal year. We can, however, observe what Africa has accomplished over the last 25-plus years as a starting point to understand why China has piled into Africa with such abandon. Understanding why Africa has great potential also has important implications for whether U.S. companies should take a new — or perhaps first — look at the continent.

This monograph argues that the continent's improved political governance, macroeconomic stability, microeconomic reforms, and increased globalization have been more important to Africa's growth surge since 2000 than have higher commodity prices:

- *Improved Political Governance*: Greater accountability from democratically elected governments brings the hope of longer-term stability and economic growth less impeded by the systemic corruption of the past. African countries were freed from the clientilism of the Cold War period after the Berlin Wall fell in 1989 and the Soviet Union collapsed in 1991, setting off a multiyear wave of political liberalization that started with Benin's national conference in 1990.[54] Since then, there has been a peace dividend in Africa, since the average number of serious conflicts recorded each year has nearly halved, from 4.8 in the 1990s to 2.6 in the 2000s.[55] The Arab Spring of popular demonstrations in Tunisia, Egypt, and Libya led in 2011 to the overturning of decades of autocratic rule in North Africa. While events in Somalia have, to greater and lesser degrees, destabilized much of the Horn of Africa, the political situation in Sub-Saharan Africa on the whole has improved, with several regional conflicts being gradually resolved. In West Africa, for example, civil wars in Liberia and Sierra Leone ended in recent years, and security sector reform has been undertaken. In 2010, Guinea and Cote d'Ivoire held democratic elections, followed sooner or later by the victors' ascent to the Presidency.

- *Improved Macroeconomic Performance*: Africa's economies grew healthier as governments reduced the average inflation rate from 22 percent in the 1990s to 8 percent after 2000. They shrank their budget deficits by two-thirds, and, helped by the Highly Indebted Poor Countries (HIPC) initiative and Paris Club reschedulings, trimmed their foreign debt by one-quarter. Average government debt as a percentage of GDP was 59 percent in the 2000s, compared with

81.9 percent in the 1990s — which means lower debt ratios than the United States and most European nations. Between 2001 and 2010, six of the 10 fastest growing economies in the world were in Africa.[56]

- *Successful Microeconomic Reforms*: Many African countries have privatized state-owned enterprises, lowered corporate taxes, strengthened regulatory and legal systems, and provided critical physical and social infrastructure. Nigeria privatized more than 116 enterprises between 1999 and 2006. It also reformed its banking sector, which went from a peak of 90 banks in the mid-2000s to 24 by the end of the decade — and a stronger sector overall.[57] Morocco and Egypt struck free-trade agreements with major export partners.

- *Increased Globalization*: Increased foreign trade has expanded welfare through greater export earnings and employment and also contributed to higher standards of living via lower-cost imports. Africa is gaining greater access to international capital: total foreign-capital flows into Africa rose from $15 billion in 2000 to a peak of $87 billion in 2007.[58] Capital inflows are forecast to reach $150 billion by 2015.[59]

Interrelated demographic and social changes are also important drivers for Africa's long-term growth. Key among these will be a growing labor force, urbanization, and the rise of the middle-class African consumer:

- *Expanding Labor Force*: In contrast with much of the world, Africa's labor force is expanding and youthful. At present, the continent has more than 500 million people of working age. By 2040, Africa will be home to one in five of the planet's young people and will have the world's largest working-age population: over 1.1 billion, more than China or India. By 2050, Africa will have one of four workers on the planet. Already, Africa's median age of 19.7 years (18.6 in Sub-Saharan Africa) is considerably younger than the 29.2 years in Asia, 36.8 years in the United States, and 40.1 years in Europe.[60] This youth bulge—whose productivity has also been aided by improvements in health and education—will also lift GDP growth. Over the last 20 years, three-quarters of the continent's increase in GDP per capita came from an expanding workforce, the rest from higher labor productivity.

- *Urbanization*: In many African countries, urbanization—with its economies of scale—is boosting productivity. In 1980, just 28 percent of Africans lived in cities. Today, this figure is 40 percent, and is projected to rise to 50 percent by 2030. Already, Africa has 52 cities with at least 1 million people.[61] Urbanization is spurring the construction of more roads, buildings, water systems, and similar projects. Since 2000, Africa's annual private infrastructure investments have tripled, averaging $19 billion from 2006 to 2008. By 2030, the continent's top 18 cities could have a combined annual spending power of $1.3 trillion.

- *Rise of the Middle Class*: Many Africans are joining the ranks of the world's consumers. In 2000, roughly 59 million households on the continent had $5,000 or more in income. By 2014, the number of such households could reach 106 million. By one measure, the number of middle-class Africans rose by 27 percent from 2000.[62] The number of households with discretionary income is projected to rise by 50 percent over the next 10 years, reaching 128 million.[63] If Africa maintains its current growth trajectory, consumers will buy $1.4 trillion worth of goods and services in 2020, which will be a little less than India's projected $1.7 trillion but more than Russia's $960 billion.[64]

THE PUSH WITHIN CHINA: 1993 SHIFT TO OIL IMPORTER LEADS TO LINKAGE OF AID/TRADE; 2001 WTO ACCESSION LEADS TO "GOING-OUT" POLICY

China's trade and aid in Africa from the 1950s to the late 1970s was in support of the PRC's communist, anti-colonial ideology. Since then, however, there have been four watershed events that have shifted Beijing's approach to the African continent from the economy serving diplomacy to diplomacy serving the economy:

- 1978: Deng Xiaoping Launches "Reform and Opening Policy." Since 1978, China has moved much closer to a market economy, in which profits, not political agendas, have driven most of the economic and trade activities. Over the course of time, China's relations with African countries have also been restructured from being anti-colonial brothers-in-arms to economic and trade partners based on market principles.[65]
- 1993: Faced with declining domestic oil production and skyrocketing demand spurred by

rapid industrialization, China became a net importer of oil and began to seek diversified suppliers, including African.

- 1995: Reflecting China's need for greater natural resource inputs for industrialization, the State Council mandated that the Ministry of Commerce combine African aid, trade, and investment.[66] The State Council also directed China's state-owned companies to launch a number of trade, investment, and development centers across Africa. Each center was to be built and operated independently by an experienced Chinese company with extensive business interests in that country. In December 1995, Complant, a state-owned enterprise newly independent from the Ministry, opened the first trade, investment, and development center in Guinea. At least 10 other centers followed. Consistent with the State Council's mandate, the Ministry also directed its municipal and provincial branches to organize delegations of outstanding enterprises to travel to Africa.

- 2001: China was admitted to the WTO—a turning point in its nominal acceptance of the Western, rules-based international economic system.[67] That same year, and under the leadership of Premier and economic czar Zhu Rongji, China's 10th 5-year plan formalized the directive for Chinese companies to go global, expand into new markets, build up the country's fledgling multinational corporations, and aid its domestic restructuring by pushing mature sunset industries offshore.[68]

Another push factor has been the desire to seek higher returns on China's huge savings. In terms of portfolio theory, China has been looking for the lowest-risk, highest-return options for the recycling of China dollars that represent its huge trade surplus, much as Middle East oil producers recycled petrodollars into the world economy in the 1970s. In a certain sense, the aggressive lending by Chinese state banks in Africa, following the Chinese government's foreign policy decisions to expand commercial relations with Africa, could also be seen as a higher-risk, higher-return bet on the future of Africa, as well as part of an effort to diversify a global portfolio away from shorter-term, dollar-based financial instruments into longer-term, non-U.S. assets.

This may prove to be a smart bet for China: McKinsey Global Institute has calculated that foreign investments in Africa have yielded, on average, the highest rates of return on investment of any region—returns that are accruing increasingly to Chinese firms while U.S. firms sit on the sidelines. Furthermore, China smartly expanded its own lending and investment, continuing it during the global economic downturn in 2008—thus allowing China even better terms on new deals.

FACTORS IN CHINA'S SUCCESS IN RAPIDLY EXPANDING ECONOMIC TIES WITH AFRICA

The second "big picture" question posed about the China-Africa economic relationship is, "Why has China been so successful in expanding its economic relations with Africa?" We preview the following reasons here and then offer a more-detailed discussion below.

1. Chinese firms are becoming more globally competitive; in Africa, they offer good value for goods and services adapted to African needs and income levels.

2. China has carried out superior economic diplomacy in Africa, characterized by heads-of-state summits; high-level bilateral visits; a universal diplomatic presence; strong advocacy for bilateral trade, investment, and tax agreements; and symbolic diplomacy.

3. China has vastly expanded its soft power in Africa, including expanded scholarships and training, an international visitor program, cultural centers, and a new volunteer corps.

4. China's development assistance programs — official aid, preferential trade credits, and development finance — are all tied to China's commercial interests, but divorced from political/governance issues (with the exception of supporting Beijing's "One China" policy). China's assistance is consistent with its mercantilist, state-led development model, but it runs contrary to international/OECD aid norms and free rides on HIPC and Paris Club debt relief.

5. China's already internationally competitive construction sector has benefited greatly from a renewed emphasis among donors and African governments on building infrastructure, winning international and national tenders, as well as associated aid contracts from its own government — the significant majority of which are infrastructure-related.

6. Chinese firms, both large and small, come from a business culture in China where bribery is endemic. Combined with African countries where corruption is rampant, and not constrained by the OECD's anti-bribery convention, Chinese firms have been hyper-shrewd at deal making.

Chinese Firms Are Becoming Globally Competitive.

China is not the "world's factory" for nothing. Before a discussion of a series of what may appear to be harsh criticisms of Chinese government policies and business practices, it is important to recognize that Chinese firms are becoming better and better at what they do. Just over 10 years after Beijing started its "going-out" policy, more and more Chinese companies are competing successfully in Africa and have established the distribution and service channels that will poise them for further success. When I arrived in Lubumbashi in 1987 to start my Foreign Service career at the U.S. Consulate-General there, I was told that the last Chinese restaurant in town had closed a few months before—a sure sign that the region's mining industry had hit hard times. The relatively few Chinese products visible in the marketplace were decidedly low tech: cheap enamelware for food products and household plastic products. Today, the Chinese have returned to Lubumbashi in force, as Chinese firms have invested heavily in mining operations in Katanga Province, while Chinese consumer products, from electronics to cars, are everywhere.

The main competitive advantage of most Chinese companies vis-à-vis Western and other Asian producers is their lower costs, aided by the core of Beijing's mercantilist policies: a deliberately undervalued currency. For manufactured goods, this cost advantage also often comes from huge economies of scale at factories in China. For service providers in Africa, the cost advantage comes from lower labor costs. Chinese managers and engineers, for example, have lower salaries and live in more modest conditions compared with their highly compensated Western counterparts. Some Chinese companies, such as in the telecommunication and construction sectors, deliver goods and services at attractive prices because they have adapted (and in some cases stolen) technology from elsewhere and/or become experienced at what they do. Western electronic giants such as Hewlett-Packard, Motorola, Siemens, and Ericsson are increasingly losing business to Chinese telecommunication companies such as Huawei and ZTE, which were active in 2010 in 50 African countries—providing more third-generation or better networks in over 30 African countries, and fiber-optic networks and e-government networks in over 20 African countries.[69]

The days when U.S. firms could win large construction contracts in Africa—such as Morrison-Knudsen's contract to build the Inga-Shaba dam in the DRC in the 1970s—now seem like a distant memory. So successful have Chinese firms become in African infrastructure development that, prior to the publication of guidelines prohibiting government-owned enterprises of any nationality competing for U.S. taxpayer-funded Millennium Challenge Corporation (MCC) contracts, a Chinese state-owned engineering and construction company, Sinohydro, was awarded the two largest projects in the MCC compact with Mali: $71.6 million for improvements to the Bamako International Airport and $46.3 million for expansion of irrigation canals along the Niger River.[70]

The bottom line is that Chinese products and services have crowded out Western firms in all but the small upper-end luxury market in Africa.[71] Mthuli Ncube, Chief Economist at the African Development Bank Group, estimated that Chinese firms accounted for 40 percent of the corporate contracts signed in Africa in 2010, versus only 2 percent for U.S. firms.[72] Not surprisingly, the lightning-fast expansion of Chinese interests in Africa has led to strong criticism, particularly in Western venues where the loss of the continent as a private "chasse gardée" is eyed jealously.[73]

China's Superior Economic Diplomacy with Africa.

A second competitive advantage of Chinese companies is that Beijing's official assistance to its companies in Africa has been multifaceted and, taken together, clearly superior to that provided by Western governments. As noted, in 1995, China's State Council directed its Commerce Ministry to revamp its Africa policy, emphasizing the linkage between aid and trade. By the late 1990s, the most senior leadership in China's government and Communist party began to involve itself directly in the country's economic diplomacy with Africa. Five key characteristics of Chinese economic diplomacy in Africa include:

a. Heads-of-State Summits: The Forum on China-Africa Cooperation (FOCAC) is the embodiment of China's new, higher-level political engagement with Africa. This heads-of-state forum, which was modeled along the lines of the Franco-African summit process, started with an initial conference in Beijing in 2000. The second, third, fourth, and fifth triennial FOCACs were held in 2003, 2006, 2009, and 2012 respectively, in Addis Ababa (Ethiopia), Beijing, Sharm El Sheikh (Egypt), and again in Beijing. Through FOCAC, Beijing has set out 3-year engagement plans toward the continent in the form of strategic initiatives and commitments—"deliverables" amounting to multi-billions of dollars in aid and investment. The PRC's "state capitalism" approach is unique in that the government is able to make sweeping pronouncements often on behalf of its business sector to invest and commit capital to Africa. This is possible only because of the political economy of China, wherein the government is still able to maintain direct control over key sectors of its economy and leading state-owned companies.[74]

One African minister responsible for economic affairs told me in November 2011 that the United States should stop complaining about China's commercial successes in Africa and start promoting its own business interests more effectively.[75] One reason for China's success, he explained, was that Beijing's leaders were far more attentive to the need to court African leaders. At FOCAC Summits, China's leaders spend 2 full days with all African heads of state. The Indians have also started inviting African heads of state to their own summits (in New Delhi in April 2008, and Addis Ababa in May 2011), the minister noted, so why not the United States?

b. Personal Diplomacy with African Elites through High-Level Bilateral Visits: China has also based its foreign diplomacy in Africa principally, but not exclusively, on establishing personal relationships with African elites. Again, the PRC's modus operandi is similar to that of France, in that foreign policymakers in Paris have built relations with former colonies in Africa around a network of personal ties with individual African leaders, bolstered by a web of bilateral agreements in trade, finance, development assistance, and defense.[76] The style of PRC diplomacy with Africa reflects Chinese culture, with its emphasis on rank, personal connections, and "face" and gift-giving. This style is also particularly effective in Africa because of its similarity to African cultural norms, including, unfortunately, baksheesh — the willingness to give and insistence on receiving bribes as "gifts."

The Chinese leadership has been politically dexterous in the way it courts African leaders. China's President, Hu Jintao, has made six trips to multiple African countries—two as vice president and four as president. President Hu Jintao and Prime Minister Wen Jiabao have visited more than two dozen African countries, and made visits to Africa as least three times as often as Presidents Bush and Obama.[77] Each year since 1991, China's foreign minister has made his first visit abroad to an African country. Consistent with this, in January 2012, Foreign Minister Yang Jiechi visited Cote d'Ivoire, Niger, and Namibia. In their interactions with African leaders, Chinese officials repeatedly stress the "win-win" rhetoric of a partnership with "mutual respect, equality, and mutual benefit."[78] By holding political and business summits such as the various Sino-African forums and arranging state visits by high-ranking Chinese political officials, Beijing symbolically accords Africa equal diplomatic status with the dominant world powers. For their part, African elites are deeply appreciative of being given the red carpet treatment whenever they turn up in Beijing.[79]

Moreover, China has another layer of high-level contacts—senior Communist Party of China officials—that frequently visit Africa to expand relations with African party and executive branch officials. The United States has no similar counterpart, nor does it rely as heavily on presidential and vice presidential visits to Africa. If you exclude annual visits to UN headquarters in New York by African leaders, where some do have meetings with the American President, Chinese leaders extend far more invitations to African leaders to visit China than the United States does to visit Washington. Additionally, the Communist Party of China frequently invites leaders of African political parties to visit China.[80] In the March 2012 testimony before Congress, the President of the Corporate Council on Africa put it this way:

> China understands the importance of Africa to its future. . . . The most important Chinese government officials visit Africa annually and they send many delegations of Chinese leaders to Africa every year. One need only note that the last visit of a U.S. Secretary of Commerce to Africa was in 2002 to understand the implications of this.[81]

PRC national Yun Sun, Visiting Fellow at the Brookings Institution's Northeast Asia Policy Studies program, asserted at a November 2011 conference that Africa was not important to Chinese national interests. One clear indicator of this, she stated, was the fact that the Chinese Communist Party's Politburo Standing Committee (of nine members) had held only two meetings in the last 4 years specifically about Africa: one related to Darfur, and the second about the evacuation of some 30,000 Chinese nationals from Libya in March 2011.[82] Comments like this should be taken with a grain of salt: senior Chinese leaders regularly travel to Africa, and receive African leaders in Beijing. African nations may be relatively less high profile to Beijing, but they are important to China nonetheless — and increasingly so.

   c. PRC's "Universal" Diplomatic Presence in Africa; Taiwan Loses Battle of "Dollar Diplomacy": China has diplomatic relations with 50 of the 54 African countries. Only four smaller nations — Burkina Faso, Swaziland, Gambia, and São Tomé and Principe — recognize Taipei. Beijing has an embassy in all but one of these 50 countries. The exception is Somalia, where the security situation in Mogadishu precludes a physical presence. All 50 African countries that recognize China, except the Comoros and the recently independent South Sudan, also have embassies in Beijing, [83] often in chanceries provided by the Chinese government. China's "universal" presence in Africa — and the support to Chinese business that flows from them — is one more reason why the United States should not be tempted to close any embassies in Africa, regardless of current budgetary difficulties.

d. Protecting China's Trade, Investment, and Tax Interests in Africa: China has carried out active economic diplomacy in Africa to protect its commercial interests. The Chinese government has established 11 Trade Promotion Centers.[84] This expansion contrasts sharply with the U.S. Department of Commerce, which has closed some of its offices in Africa in recent years. Beijing has also signed bilateral trade agreements with 45 African countries, bilateral investment treaties with 33 African countries, and double taxation agreements with 11 African countries.[85] According to the 12th Five-Year Plan, China will continue to promote agreements with African governments for the protection of investments and the avoidance of double taxation.[86]

e. Symbolic Diplomacy: Prestige projects have also played an important part in securing agreements with African governments, and African capitals throughout the continent are filled with stadiums and government buildings built by China. This form of symbolic diplomacy has great appeal to African elites, who welcome the opportunity to replace colonial-era buildings.[87] As the African Union (AU) matured and grew in importance as an institution following its founding in 2002, Beijing cleverly exercised the ultimate act of symbolic diplomacy: the donation to the AU of a new,

800-million-renminbi (RMB) ($124 million) headquarters building, which was inaugurated in January 2012.

How should the U.S. Government respond to China's superior economic diplomacy? One option would be to raise the level of its engagement with Africa, making it less episodic and more sustained. This could start at the top. For example, the next U.S. President could personally host a U.S.-Africa Summit for Heads of State, much as is done already by France, China, and India. U.S. Cabinet members, such as the Commerce, Energy, and Treasury Secretaries, could make more frequent visits to the continent, accompanied by U.S. business delegations. Better funding for the U.S. Export-Import Bank, the Overseas Private Insurance Corporation (OPIC), and the Trade Development Administration (TDA) is another obvious answer. The United States could better fund the Department of Commerce's Foreign Commercial Service (FCS), or even return it to the State Department, where it was originally located until 1979.[88] The State Department, through its embassies in Africa, has an on-the-ground presence in virtually all African capitals and a handful of constituent posts, and thus, has a far greater network of offices on the continent than does FCS. (The United States has embassies in every country in Africa except for the two island nations of Comoros and Seychelles, narco-state Guinea-Bissau, and war-torn Somalia; China has embassies in every country where it has diplomatic relations [four still maintain ties with Taiwan] except Somalia.) However, the U.S. Department of Commerce maintains U.S. Commercial Service Offices in only eight African countries, three of which are in North Africa, while the Chinese Ministry of Commerce has Commercial Counselors in 48 of its Embassies in Africa.[89]

Commercial diplomacy should be made an explicit part of the promotion criteria for all State Department Foreign Service Officers (FSOs), with mandatory training in commercial advocacy provided to all Ambassadors, Deputy Chiefs of Missions, and Economic/Commercial officers before they arrive at Post. U.S. Secretary of State Hillary Clinton's October 14, 2011, speech was an excellent statement of the importance of economic statecraft to the United States, but the key will be action, including a fundamental change in the mindset of the U.S. Foreign Service—it must come to understand, like the Chinese—that national strength ultimately depends on economic strength and that commercial advocacy is thus central to the work of U.S. diplomats. As Secretary Clinton put it:

> Our foreign and economic relations remain indivisible. Only now, our great challenge is not deterring any single military foe, but advancing our global leadership at a time when power is more often measured and exercised in economic terms.

China Boosting Its Soft Power in Africa.

A third reason for China's newly found success in Africa is its expanded development and use of soft power. Since the first FOCAC Summit in 2000, China has made a systematic effort to expand its soft power policies in Africa.[90] This soft power builds goodwill and minimizes possible negative reactions on the continent to the growing influence of its corporations and citizens. If China's summit- and relationship-based diplomacy in Africa was learned from France, several elements of its soft power diplomacy are lifted from the U.S. diplomatic playbook:

- Scholarships, Training: China's training of Africans, including diplomats and journalists, is a part of its soft power diplomacy. At the 2009 FOCAC Summit, China announced its intention to increase to 4,000 the number of full scholarships it offers to African students each year.[91] Beijing even funds sports teams and provides equipment for aspiring African Olympians.[92]
- Cultural Centers: In 2001, China had only four cultural centers attached to its embassies in Africa, including one in Cotonou, Benin. Ten years later, there are at least 22 Confucius Institutes in 19 countries in Africa that focus on teaching Chinese language, culture, and history, and the number continues to grow.
- News Media Influence: China is increasing its radio transmissions to Africa in various languages, has set up a transmitting facility in Kenya, and has rebroadcast arrangements with countries around the continent. In January 2012, China Central TV (CCTV) started English-language news broadcasts to Africa from its new studios in Nairobi, Kenya, with programs such as "Africa Live," "Talk Africa," and "Faces of Africa." CCTV hopes to build a network of 14 news bureaus in Africa and, by 2015, broadcast 24 hours a day to the continent.[93] The Xinhua news service has more than 20 bureaus in Africa and regional offices in Cairo and Nairobi. Xinhua competes directly with Reuters, AP, and Bloomberg for reporting on events in Africa. A number of sources for this monograph were based on Xinhua reporting.
- Volunteer Corps: More recently, Beijing has expanded its foreign assistance program in Africa

to include a Chinese volunteer youth corps, mirroring services of the U.S. Peace Corps.[94]

- International Visitor Programs: Historically, the United States has identified young emerging African leaders, both political and economic, for exchange programs in the United States under the "International Visitors Program." China is now doing the same thing — identifying members of parliament, local entrepreneurs, and well-placed government officials in such key ministries as Foreign Affairs, Internal Affairs, and Trade and Commerce for training and exchange programs in Beijing.[95]

Beijing's Development Assistance: Mercantilist, Governance Neutral, and a Tool for China's Economic and Political Diplomacy.

A fourth factor in China's economic success in Africa is that Beijing's official aid, preferential trade credits, and development finance have been both mercantilist, i.e., tied to Chinese commercial interests, and governance neutral — not tied to specific African government policies (except the "One China" policy). As such, these policies pose a fundamental challenge to existing norms governing international aid architecture. Existing international norms are embodied in the OECD Development Assistance Committee (DAC) guidelines, which have emphasized transparency, with conditionality tied only to good governance (and not to the providing nation's goods and services).[96] In sharp contrast, China's aid, export credit, and development finance policies are opaque and tied to the purchase of Chinese goods and services.[97] One American scholar defended China's aid policies, writing that "China may wind up supporting some dictatorial and corrupt regimes, but—and this is an inconvenient truth—the West also supports such regimes when it advances its interests."[98] But this view ignores the fact that the United States also raises human rights issues with all regimes, including China and all nations of Africa, admittedly more discreetly with oil-rich countries such as Equatorial Guinea, but also very publicly in a blunt annual human rights report for each country. Obviously, China does not do this.

China's export-promotion policies have come under fire for allegedly using cheap credit to provide its goods and services exporters with an unfair advantage in staking out a dominant position in Africa.[99] Critics assert that Beijing's zero- or low-interest export credits violate OECD rules—an accusation that would be valid, except that China is not a member of that organization and thus has no obligation to follow its rules. Under the voluntary 1978 Arrangement on Officially Supported Export Credits, concessional export credits from OECD governments were supposed to be limited to projects that were not commercially viable: the construction of public goods like primary schools or health clinics.[100] China EXIM Bank's website stresses that its export buyer's credits generally follow the Arrangement, even though China is not an OECD member.

Whether fair or not, China has vastly expanded the amount of export credit and development finance targeting Africa, and this is helping to fuel Chinese firms' success on the continent. China's cumulative foreign aid of $11.5 billion since the 1950s has already been surpassed by loans from China EXIM Bank to Africa, which were $5 billion from 2007 to 2009 alone. China EXIM's cumulative loans to Africa are expected to total $20 billion by 2012. For its part, China Development Bank said in September 2010 that it had already disbursed $5.6 billion to 35 projects in more than 30 African countries, and made cumulative commitments of over $10 billion.[101]

China announced at the Fourth FOCAC Ministerial Conference, held in November 2009 in Egypt, that it would provide $10 billion of preferential loans to Africa from 2010 to 2012. According to a 2010 State Council White Paper, this will be composed of $3 billion in preferential loans, $2 billion in preferential export buyer's credits, and $5 billion toward the establishment of the China-Africa Development Fund, which is designed to encourage and support Chinese companies investing in projects in Africa. The White Paper said that examples of major projects that will receive preferential credits include an airport in Mauritius, housing in Equatorial Guinea, and the Bui Hydropower Station in Ghana. The White Paper also indicated that China would provide credits of up to $1 billion to Chinese financial institutions for the development of small and medium enterprises (SMEs) in Africa.[102]

China's Aid Positive As Well: Emphasis on Infrastructure Investments Fills Important Development Gap.

A fifth factor in China's success in Africa has been its emphasis on building infrastructure, which has been a boon to China's already internationally competitive construction industry. The World Bank has estimated that Africa needs $20 billion in infrastructure investments annually, and has a shortfall of about $10 billion a year.[103] Some academics, and some African leaders such as former President of Mozambique Joaquim Chissano, have blamed the West for worsening this gap in African infrastructure needs by singularly focusing on social development needs, as exemplified by UN Millennium Development Goals (MDGs) negotiated in 2000. Whatever the case, Africans themselves recognized the need for more infrastructure in formulating their New Partnership for Africa's Development (NEPAD) in 2001, and China — which kicked off its "going-out" policy that same year — was ready to help fill Africa's infrastructure shortfall.

Over the last 10 years, China has become the major builder in Africa, winning international contracts and dedicating much of its own aid to infrastructure projects. "China is able to build a railway before the World Bank would get around to doing a cost-benefit analysis," one Western diplomat said.[104] After Liberia's war ended, President Johnson Sirleaf repeatedly said that her number one priority was getting roads financed. According to adviser Steven Radelet, "No one was doing it. They all said 'we don't do roads'. But the Chinese ambassador said: 'We'll do roads'."

Worldwide, over 60 percent of China EXIM Bank's concessional loans have been committed to infrastructure projects, and this percentage is likely similar or higher for its credits to Africa.[105] U.S. Senator Chris Coons, who chairs the Senate Foreign Relations Subcommittee on African Affairs, estimated in November 2011 that about 70 percent of Chinese assistance to Africa comes in the form of roads, stadiums, and government buildings — often built with Chinese material and labor — while 70 percent of U.S. Government spending there goes on crucial but less visible support for people, particularly to fight HIV/AIDS, malaria, tuberculosis, and other diseases.[106]

According to China's State Council, by the end of 2009, Beijing had provided assistance for the construction of over 500 infrastructure projects in Africa.[107] In recent years, China has signed loan agreements with Angola for about $14.5 billion (2004 and later) and the DRC for $6.5 billion (2009) — many of which were infrastructure-related. In September 2010, China and Ghana signed loans valued at about $15 billion. Most of this money will be used to finance roads, dams, refineries, buildings, railways, etc., by Chinese construction companies, and some will be repaid in oil or minerals.[108] The China-Africa Development Fund (CADF) provided a $100 million loan to assist Ethiopia to complete a railway networking system that links Addis Ababa to various regions of the country.[109] The China Development Bank (CDB) is to fund construction of a cement factory in Mozambique's Maputo Province, costing $100 million.

China's emphasis on infrastructure has paid huge dividends. China has become the hydropower, road, rail, and bridge builder of Africa. In 2008, Chinese companies had nearly 3,000 engineering contracts in Africa, valued at close to $40 billion.[110] Some 187,396 Chinese were officially working in Africa in 2009, most on the large engineering contracts in Algeria, Libya, and Angola. Although there are exceptions, such as Angola, most of China's engineering business in Africa is not actually financed by the Chinese government, but by African governments, development banks, bilateral banks, and private companies contracting with Chinese firms. Including contracts for the private sector and international community, Chinese companies now earn revenues of over $20 billion annually from construction and engineering contracts on the continent.

In other words, the Chinese not only believe in integrating aid and trade into their own development assistance policy, but also in taking advantage as much as possible of the untied aid provided by other countries and the international financial institutions. Since China does not accede to OECD DAC rules, it enjoys the free ride of taking advantage of the West's negotiated policies of untying aid without providing reciprocal access to Western construction companies to Beijing's aid contracts. In fairness, the Chinese are also strong at providing internationally competitive construction and engineering services, and win a significant share of open tenders carried out according to international norms. The Africans themselves win both from China's tied aid, and from Chinese construction companies providing badly needed infrastructure with the least amount of development aid.

Corruption, Flouting of Labor, Environmental Laws: China's Illicit Competitive Advantages in Africa.

In a sense, the sixth factor in China's success in Africa is its most corrosive: illegal behavior such as the use of bribery and corruption to advance its political and economic interests, and the flouting of labor and environmental laws to lower its cost of doing business. Chinese state-owned enterprises, private corporations, and individual citizens are systematically using corruption, a form of cumshaw, to win business deals in Africa, and are not subject to restrictions such as Washington's Foreign Corrupt Practices Act. Since under-the-table transactions are inherently hard to prove, we can only assert that:

- Corruption is endemic at all levels in China, a societal problem against which the Communist Party inveighs regularly because it represents a serious source of social discontent and thus a threat to the Party's continued hold on power;
- Chinese companies transfer their corrupt practices abroad, including a gift-giving culture of corruption that is ingrained in China's business culture.

Not surprisingly, Chinese companies are the second most likely (after India) to use payola abroad, according to Transparency International's Bribe Payers Index. In terms of African partners, a World Bank survey of 68 countries in 2007 found that Sub-Saharan Africa leads in the "percentage of firms expected to give gifts" to secure government contracts. This corrupt meeting of the minds has facilitated China's "hyper-efficient deal making in Africa," as one observer put it.[111]

The poster child for questionable Chinese business practices in Africa may belong to a firm dubbed the "Queensway Syndicate," which was founded by well-connected Cantonese entrepreneurs.[112] This syndicate, with its African partners, has signed contracts worth billions of dollars for oil, minerals, and diamonds from Africa. Operating out of offices in Hong Kong's Queensway, the syndicate calls itself China International Fund, or China Sonangol. Almost all of China's imports of oil from Angola — worth more than $20 billion last year — come from China Sonagol. The son of Angolan President Dos Santos is said to be a director of China Sonangol. According to the IMF and World Bank, billions of dollars have disappeared from Sonangol's accounts. In Guinea, the syndicate came to the rescue of the military junta then in power, with a reported transfer of funds of $100 million. The junta eventually fell, however, and following the first democratic elections in Guinea's 50-year history in 2010, the syndicate's $7 billion minerals deal is now in limbo.

Sometimes a corruption problem becomes so high profile that Beijing's Foreign Ministry officials feel compelled to repudiate actions that China's increasingly independent public and private enterprises take, such as the Queensway minerals deal in 2007 with the increasingly isolated military regime in Guinea.[113] There were news reports in 2011 of similar problems, with arms sales by Chinese state-owned enterprises (SOEs) to the failing Qaddafi regime in Libya.

Many Africans assert that the practices of Chinese companies are not all that different from the practices of European investors.[114] While this may have been true in the past for Europeans, it is certainly less so now. Most European nations have signed on to the OECD anti-bribery agreement that was championed in the 1990s by the United States. This agreement, as implemented by each member-state, provides for fines and even criminal penalties for firms that pay bribes abroad. While bribery by some Western firms undoubtedly continues, the OECD anti-bribery convention has likely reduced corruption by Western firms, thereby serving up another competitive advantage for Chinese companies that are not bound by this convention and feel no compunction over giving bribes, especially in Africa, where the chances of being caught and punished are almost nonexistent.

Without improved governance at home, China, its companies, and its citizens will continue to be opportunistic, exploiting weaker African nation-states in their quest for markets and profits.[115] Former South

African President Thabo Mbeki, whose country is both a strategic competitor and partner of China, felt compelled to publicly state just after a FOCAC summit that the continent should beware of trading traditional Western modes of dominance for a Chinese version.[116] Africa's elites must thus act wisely on behalf of their citizenry, with an eye toward mutual benefit that defends their own countries' interests with fairness to China. Zambian President Michael Sata, who was elected in September 2011, will hopefully be one such wise leader. He used anti-Chinese slogans in two presidential campaigns, and was elected on his second try. While calling for a rise in the minimum wage in an attempt to resolve a strike against Chinese firms that occurred shortly after his taking office, President Sata also moved quickly to reassure some investors about previous campaign slogans. His first meeting with a foreign official after being elected was with the Chinese Ambassador in Lusaka—whom Sata reportedly reassured about his welcoming of Chinese investment.[117]

ARE AFRICA'S NEW DEBTS TO CHINA SUSTAINABLE?

A third "big-picture" question posed is whether China is creating a new debt burden for Africa. China's massive trade surpluses and capital reserves provided Africa with a new ability to offer large-scale finance, just as African countries were finally successful in getting multilateral debt relief through the HIPC program.[118] While most Africans welcome China's emergence as a major creditor, many Western observers warn that Chinese banks—consistent with Beijing's mercantilist philosophy—are "free-riding" on the debt-reduction generosity of Western donors by extending new loans to low-income countries. These observers assert that Beijing has created a wave of new debt that is only minimally offset by the debts that China has forgiven in some African countries.[119] Moreover, since Chinese loans lack transparency, it is impossible for outsiders to understand how they fit into the African borrower's debt sustainability frameworks developed with the IMF and World Bank.[120] Chinese Premier Wen Jiabao announced in November 2009 that China planned to cancel 168 debts owed by 33 African countries, but did not announce the total amount of this proposed debt relief.[121]

China EXIM Bank President and CEO Li Ruogu has argued that his bank takes into consideration both debt and development sustainability in making lending decisions in Africa.[122] As the EXIM Bank's chief economist told an audience at a World Bank retreat: "It's the new lenders' problem if countries can't repay, not the Paris Club. We know we need a good, strong balance sheet."

One important way that China mitigates the risk of its loans is by tying its provision of credit to a commodity offtake agreement in the contracting African country—a technique commonly referred to as the "Angola Model." Under this technique, the borrowing country agrees to pay back the loan in the form of the sale of commodities, such as oil, that it produces. China's EXIM Bank has pledged oil-backed financing of some $14.5 billion for the Angolan government's ambitious post-war reconstruction program, including over 100 projects in the areas of energy, water, health, education, telecommunications, fisheries, and public works.[123] These projects are predominantly (70 percent) undertaken by Chinese contractors.[124] There are signs that the limits of this model may have been reached, however, at least within Angola. Some Angolans have complained that the infrastructure-for-oil deals with China have shackled their oil revenues to repaying Chinese loans. As a result, the government is looking to limit its exposure to further oil-backed loans with the Chinese.[125]

It appears that China's trade credits and development loans are being used productively in most countries, which suggests that these new debts will not create an unsustainable burden. One such country is Ghana. Ghana's fortunes changed when Tullow Oil struck oil in June 2007. Not coincidentally, 2 months later, the China Export Bank (CEB) signed an agreement with Ghana extending a hybrid package of $270 million in concessional loans and $292 million in export buyers' credits to fund the Bui Dam, a hydroelectric project with an anticipated capacity of 400 MW. The loan was arranged to be paid back over a period of 20 years with cocoa exports.[126] During President John Atta Mills's state visit to China in September 2010, an agreement was signed with Chinese financial institutions for almost $13 billion more in loans to Ghana. Some $3 billion in loans extended by CDB will be used to develop the country's oil and gas infrastructure, and $9.77 billion channeled toward roads, railways, schools, and hospitals.

One way that China is providing capital to Africa without adding to the continent's debt load is by making equity investments. For example, the China Africa Development Fund is an equity investor with the Government of Ghana and Bosai Minerals Group in a Sekondi industrial estate that will be anchored by a proposed aluminum refinery. Ghana has long been a producer of bauxite, mined by large Western firms.

As Ghana's Minister of Trade and Industry put it, the Chinese project "will allow our country to finally achieve our long-term objective of establishing an integrated aluminium industry and make the most of our resources."[127]

Ghana may also be an example of how infrastructure loans such as those offered by China can act as an agency of restraint in poor, resource-rich countries by ensuring that at least some of these countries' natural resource wealth is spent on development investments.[128] In other words, African countries opt to invest in their infrastructure — usually a good investment in the productivity of an economy — and make sure that it can pay back this debt by committing itself to offtake agreements involving its exportable commodities. (As discussed below, these offtake agreements can raise special economic and security concerns when they involve strategic minerals.)

At the same time, Chinese loans can also subvert the discipline that African countries might accept under their own country development plans worked out with the assistance of the IMF and World Bank. In 2004, Angola suddenly broke off negotiations with the IMF, characterizing its conditions as "humiliating" and announced that China's EXIM Bank had agreed to give Angola a $2 billion line of credit to be repaid over 12 years.[129] Paul Wolfowitz, former head of the World Bank, was strongly critical of the Chinese role in Chad, where a carefully negotiated loan by the Bank aimed at ensuring that a portion of resources would be diverted to poverty reduction had been summarily scrapped by the government after promises of Chinese credit.[130]

China's new trade credits and development loans could allow Africans to make wise investments in their future, or be diverted to questionable projects that allow elites to abandon efforts to improve governance. Which choice to make ultimately falls to African leaders.

WILL AFRICA BE ABLE TO INDUSTRIALIZE BECAUSE OF OR DESPITE CHINA?

One of the key issues surrounding China's rapidly expanding economic footprint in Africa is whether the Chinese will ultimately help—or hurt—chances for Africa to lift incomes through industrialization. Will Africa's modest progress in industrialization be gutted by competition from China, e.g., in textiles; or will Africa become more competitive, perhaps with the help of FDI, including Chinese companies relocated from the PRC to lower-cost locations in Africa?

The impediments to African industrialization are mainly within Africa itself. While the image of Africa is of extremely low wages, Africa's diversified economies actually have higher unit-labor costs—defined as wages divided by labor productivity—than do China or India. Even when factories in certain countries in Africa are as productive as those in China and India, overall costs tend to be higher because of corruption, burdensome regulation, and poor infrastructure.[131] Africa's share of labor-intensive manufacturing is actually shrinking, according to a July 2011 UN report. The World Bank has talked with Chinese trade officials on how to move more factories to Africa from China. The Bank estimates that there are now 85 million manufacturing jobs suitable for unskilled workers in China, out of a population of 1.3 billion, but only 10 million in all of Africa, with a population of 1 billion.[132]

Despite Africa's higher costs, there is increasing anecdotal evidence that China is a net boon to African industrialization. A PRC government survey of 1,600 Chinese companies indicated that they were increasingly using Africa as an industrial base, sometimes because countries have made industrial investment a precondition for resource deals. Manufacturing's share of total Chinese investment in Africa (22 percent) is catching up fast with mining's (29 percent).

In some parts of Africa—notably Nigeria and East Africa—manufacturing has become a key sector for Chinese investment.[133] Chinese home appliance giant, Haier, joined with a firm linked to the Greek diaspora in West Africa in a joint venture in Lagos, Nigeria, to assemble ozone-friendly refrigerators. Chinese investment is helping to rejuvenate plastics manufacturing in the northern Nigerian city of Kano.[134] In East Africa, Chery Automobile is to become the second Chinese vehicle maker to build an assembly plant in Kenya, joining truck manufacturer Beiqi Foton Motors.[135] The firm is discussing $50 million in loans with the Chinese government to invest in Kenya through an assembly plant. The new assemblers are looking to use Kenya as the launching pad for entry into the regional common market, the East African Community (EAC). The fragmented economies of the five East African countries had discouraged auto producers from setting up assembly plants, but the common market has made it possible for the producers to capture a regional market of more than 130 million residents. The firm sold a modest 120 cars last year, but aims to produce 1,000 units in 2013. In Ethiopia, two out of three resident Chinese firms are manufacturers.[136] One of China's leaders in telecom, ZTE, announced a joint venture in mobile phone assembly in Ethiopia, where Chinese companies are also investing in pharmaceuticals.[137]

Backward/Forward Integration of Mining Sector.

New evidence suggests that China's investments in extractive industries could enable African businesses to develop more sophisticated backward and forward integration so as to extract more value from processing.[138] Chinese investments in extractive industries in Africa are profitable, and have led to downstream processing, such as refining of copper ore in Zambia. Some African manufactured products, such as aluminum, could become a viable export to China and third markets.

Upstream Factors for Construction Sector.

Many Chinese companies initially came to Africa to win and carry out construction contracts offered by African governments, bilateral donors, and international financial institutions such as the World Bank and ADB. Beyond building infrastructure, some Chinese construction companies have promoted African industrialization through the building of upstream factories to produce cement, bricks, glass, steel rods, and other building materials.

Infrastructure Improvements Aid Industrialization.

Recently, many African countries, particularly in the EAC, have taken new steps to advance regional economic integration. China has also contributed indirectly to regional integration in Africa, and thus, the continent's prospects for industrialization, through its heavy investment in infrastructure — often made in conjunction with natural resource investments in mining sectors.

Restructuring of the Chinese Economy May Benefit Africa.

Africa may already be benefitting modestly from China's own economic restructuring. China, "the world's factory," would like to move up the value-added chain to higher-technology products, and shift away from labor-intensive, low-tech, and high-pollution industries. Rapidly rising labor costs in China's coastal provinces have already led to a massive shift in manufacturing to inland provinces such as Sichuan. However, wages have also been rising in inland provinces, and China is reaching a tipping point, where it is no longer competitive globally for certain labor-intensive goods. World Bank President Robert Zoellick advised China to ship some manufacturing abroad — something that some Chinese businesses have already started to do out of economic necessity and tightening environmental rules. Since 2005, for example, Beijing and prosperous local municipalities have progressively tightened the structure of taxes, tariffs, prohibitions, and incentives to force restructuring in the heavily polluting leather industry. One of Wenzhou's most prominent private companies, Hazan Shoes, invested $6 million in 2004 to set up a factory in Nigeria. "Our boss wants to set up a shoe production cluster, to bring the entire value chain to Nigeria," one Chinese businessman said.[139]

About the same time that China's government ramped up policies to encourage its emerging manufacturing phenoms to expand overseas, it also began encouraging less competitive, labor-intensive "mature" industries (such as textiles and leather goods) to relocate to other countries.[140] In July 2006, the Ministries of Finance and Commerce established a special fund that Chinese textile companies could draw on to encourage more of them to move offshore.

African Textiles Should Have Local Value Chain, But Chinese Competition Tough.

The issue of Africa's broader participation in global value chains is critical. One promising area for this ought to be in the cotton-textile-garment value chain, which is widely seen as the stepladder for Sub-Saharan Africa's industrial growth.[141] Africa needs to start processing local raw materials into finished goods for export rather than exporting raw cotton and cloth.[142] The problem up to now has been the high costs of production for Africa's textile industry and fierce international competition, particularly from China.

Chinese textile exports do vie with—and usually crowd out—African exports in third-country markets such as the United States and the EU.[143] With the end of the Multifibre Agreement in 2005, African producers that had established burgeoning industries in textiles and apparel, buoyed by the preferential terms of trade established by the African Growth and Opportunity Act (AGOA), were rapidly swamped by Chinese competition.[144] Even in the case of South Africa, which has a relatively advanced economy, Chinese textile imports were crushing their South African competitors, leading the Chinese to agree in 2007 to a "voluntary" quotas on textile exports to South Africa. This measure ultimately failed, however, because other Asian textile exporters, e.g., Vietnam, filled the gap left by declining Chinese exports. The ultimate solution for the South African textile industry is thus to boost its productivity, or suffer collapse in the face of global competition.

Nigeria faced a similar dilemma after 2005 because of Chinese textile imports. Nigerian manufacturers faced higher costs, notably in energy and transport, and were unable to compete. Yet, their difficulties ultimately proved to be domestic, linked to the chronic inefficiency, misadministration, and corruption within Nigeria's service industries. Similarly, one Chinese investor complained about the challenges of manufacturing in Tanzania: an irregular out-of-phase electricity supply, which damages machinery; inadequate water supply; high costs of nonlabor inputs such as raw materials; and poor industrial relations.[145]

Special Economic Zones: Can Lessons Learned by China Mitigate Weaknesses in Africa's Investment Climate?

China experimented with foreign investment, at first in a limited number of Special Economic Zones (SEZs) in its coastal provinces, where the central, provincial, and even municipal governments built infrastructure (industrial parks, roads, ports, etc.) and offered tax holidays to induce foreign investors to come. Beijing started four SEZs in 1980, one in Fujian Province, and three in Guangdong Province, including one at Shenzhen, just outside of Hong Kong. These zones were phenomenally successful, and this experiment was expanded to other coastal and later inland provinces.

At the 2006 FOCAC Summit, Beijing promised to build SEZs in several African countries to attract both Chinese and other foreign investment.[146] While development zones in China were owned by the central, provincial, or even municipal governments, and were often built and operated by separate legal entities set up for this purpose, China's "export model" for SEZs in Africa is taking the form of: 1) support and subsidies from its government, mixed with; 2) market-based decisions and investment by a combination of Chinese state-owned and private corporations. These African SEZs support China's "going-global" policies for its domestic companies, and were also part of a broader Chinese government effort to establish up to 50 overseas SEZs under the 11th Five-Year Plan (2006-10).[147] In addition to economic rationales, Beijing also had political motivations for promoting SEZs abroad. The establishment of these manufacturing zones off-sets criticism that trade with China is eroding the industrial base of its Africa trading partners, and that Chinese firms seek only to invest in Africa's extractive industries.[148] The zones may also fulfill soft power political goals by demonstrating the efficacy of aspects of China's development model.

However, China's decision to build SEZs in Africa is intended first and foremost to reduce the costs and risks of doing business for Chinese firms in Africa.[149] In theory, SEZs will act as "safe havens" for Chinese capital. Chinese (and other foreign) firms located in these zones are to enjoy tax and investment incentives, customs duty waivers for raw materials and inputs, visas and work permit approvals for expatriate labor, and discounted land and services.[150] Some SEZs even provide restrictions on strike activity.

In 2006 and 2007, China's Ministry of Commerce organized two rounds of tenders to review proposals to build six to seven SEZs in Africa. The winners of these tenders were eligible for up to 200-300 million RMB ($30-45 million) in grants, and long-term low-interest loans of RMB 2 billion ($300 million). Up to now, China has built six SEZs in five African countries. China's first two zones in Africa are being built in Zambia (at Chambishi with a projected cost of $410 million) and Mauritius (renamed Jinfei; at a cost of $720 million). Both are sponsored by Chinese companies with substantial investments in each country.[151] There are also two zones in Nigeria (Lekki; $369 million; Ogun, $500 million for the first phase), and one each in Egypt (Suez; cost N/A) and Ethiopia (Oriental, $101 million). (A seventh zone was planned for Algeria, but suspended for reasons related to unexpected changes in Algier's foreign investment laws; some consider that a subzone in Lusaka should be considered a second SEZ in Zambia.) In addition, the China Africa Development Fund (CADF), an equity fund of one of Beijing's policy banks, China Development Bank, decided to invest a total of $100 million in at least three of the zones (Nigeria Lekki, Mauritius, and Egypt).

Chinese companies developing these zones include national and provincial SOEs, but also some private firms. The zones in Ethiopia and Mauritius are 100 percent Chinese-owned, while the others are joint ventures, usually with African national or state-level governments as minority partners. For example, Nigeria's Ogun State government owns an 18 percent stake in the Ogun zone, while the government of Lagos State and an investment company it controls own 40 percent of the shares in the Lekki zone.[152] A total of $328 million had been spent to build infrastructure in these SEZs as of the end of 2010.[153]

All of the SEZs remain in the very early stages, with Egypt's Suez and Zambia's Chambishi already in partial operation, and Nigeria's Lekki aiming to be fully operational by year-end 2012. None of the zones has proceeded completely smoothly, although Zambia comes closest. Chinese developers expect host governments to support zone development actively; instead, they are finding in some projects (such as in Ethiopia) that governments allocate land to developers and do little else.[154]

Some observers are concerned that China's SEZs in Africa, instead of becoming growth nodes that partner with African companies, train local managers and workers, and catalyze local industry, will end up as enclaves without any development connection to the rest of their host countries.[155] Given Africa's weak industrial base, however, accounting for only about 1 percent of global manufacturing, a higher priority must be to make the zones attractive to foreign investors, both Chinese and third-country. In the short-to-medium term, this may mean less concern about whether Africans can maximize their immediate benefit from the zones, and more about providing inducements for new foreign investors. After all, even if the economic linkages to the rest of the country are weak, these foreign-invested factories will produce wages for local workers, build up their skills, and provide tax revenue for the state (albeit reduced at least temporarily by any tax holidays). In this regard, China's experience is instructive. The first four SEZs were created in 1980, but by 1995 "zone fever" in China had grown so intense that the central government had to put the brake on new development zones (in part to conserve arable land), and start to phase out generous tax incentives for foreign investors.

Despite the challenges, there have already been signs of success: by the end of 2011, 137 Chinese enterprises will have invested a total of $1.08 billion in the six zones. Business volume of these enterprises is predicted to reach $3.5 billion. The companies will also contribute $119 million dollars in tax revenues for local governments, while creating about 10,000 jobs.[156] Outside of these Chinese government-supported, official zones, there are a number of Chinese enterprises that have established, expanded, or proposed new industrial parks or free trade zones in Nigeria, Sierra Leone, Guinea, Uganda, Botswana, and South Africa that are independent of government support.[157]

Chinese developers experienced with zone construction in China note that even in situations in which local governments are actively facilitating a zone, it usually takes 10-15 years before a zone reaches maturity and "takes off." By way of comparison, in the United States, the Research Triangle Park in North Carolina was founded in 1959, quickly attracted two research companies, but floundered until 1965, when IBM announced it would locate a research facility there — eventually leading to the presence of 104 research companies by 1998.[158]

Too Early to Tell Impact of China on African Industrialization.

On balance, the above picture is mixed, with China playing both the role of contributor to — and competitor with — African industrialization. Because most data are limited and anecdotal, it is too early to tell whether Africa is truly poised for an industrial take-off. Between 1990 and 2005, Sub-Saharan Africa ended with an average manufacturing growth rate of just over 1.5 percent. Almost no change at all occurred in industrial structure or movement up the value chain. African industry has struggled to reach a sufficient scale to compete in global markets.

China can be a catalyst, but not a panacea for Africa's industrialization. It is possible that more and more Chinese textile companies will set up shop in Africa, joining those from other sectors who have already started to do so. How Chinese companies operate their manufacturing operations in Africa will also impact their broader contribution to African industrialization. If they cluster only in SEZs that become ghettos of restricted labor rights, walled off from contact with domestic firms, they will contribute much less to Africa's sustainable transition to industrialized economies—and will represent a tragic lost opportunity for the African countries that host them. Ultimately, however, the success of African businesses and foreign investors in manufacturing will rest not with China, but rather on the degree to which African governments establish an environment more conducive for business, thereby fostering indigenous entrepreneurial activity, as well as foreign investment from around the globe.

CHINA NOT A MONOLITH: IMPACT OF NONSTATE CHINESE ACTORS ON AFRICA

There remains a common assumption throughout Africa that all Chinese deals are state-led and orchestrated.[159] This is untrue. In analyzing Sino-African relations, we must always keep in mind that China is not a monolith—there are many Chinas and, similarly, many Africas.[160] As Chinese firms have gone abroad, there has been a steady diffusion of economic power from state-affiliated SOEs to a profit-seeking private sector; which has introduced a diversity of interests and practices that are as often at odds with Chinese foreign policy aims as they are in conformity with them.[161] Even today, some Chinese SOEs remain appendages of the government, but most have gained a very considerable degree of autonomy (although still under general and often loose supervision of national, provincial, and even municipal State Asset Administrations). Many SOEs have also been partially privatized, with companies going public on a stock exchange. As such, they come under pressure from private shareholders whose interests are not aligned with those of the State and Chinese foreign policy.

Moreover, while the Chinese leadership in Beijing may want certain outcomes from China's engagement in Africa, it is also increasingly unable to control a rapidly expanding network of state-owned and private-sector actors who have entered these markets based on the logic of globalization and profit maximization. This network, from the most "controllable" to the least, includes:

- Large Chinese enterprises investing in strategic sectors such as oil, ores, or infrastructure. Most are state-owned and/or subsidized with Chinese grants or benefit from cheap policy loans by state-owned banks;
- Medium- to large-sized Chinese companies found mainly in the manufactured goods, telecommunications, and service sectors,[162] and;
- Small firms and individual or family businesses, which are dominant in light industry, and the wholesale and retail sectors.[163]

Chinese state-owned banks such as China EXIM Bank and China Development Bank are playing increasingly large financing roles on the continent, but they still largely cater to Chinese state companies. Private Chinese companies have often complained of the lack of Chinese government support in this respect. It was in recognition of this that the Chinese government announced the launch in 2009 of a $1 billion fund geared especially toward small- and medium-sized enterprises in Africa. Although the bigger state-owned Chinese enterprises dominate the headlines with large-scale infrastructure and resource-related deals, the most dynamic sector of Chinese investment in Africa is the private entrepreneurs.

Unfortunately, and in some cases undeservedly, Chinese companies in Africa have developed a highly negative reputation for limited employment of Africans, limited technological transfer, and, in some cases, uneven workmanship. Worse still, many Chinese investors have brought with them notoriously low labor rights standards and a wholesale disregard for the environment that mimicked the pattern of accidental injuries and deaths, periodic strikes, and long-standing ecological degradation found in China itself. Construction firms in Zambia and Namibia have documented unfair Chinese business practices, including collusive bidding, low wages, and a tendency to hire contract workers so as to get around mandated labor benefits (paid holidays, sick leave, etc.) for permanent staff. To avoid censure, Chinese managers bribe union bosses and take them on "study tours" (i.e., massage parlors) in China.[164] A study by Namibian labor unions pointed out that the Chinese were following the same practices as local African firms. European-owned firms that adhered to local labor laws and regulations suffered most.[165]

Another example of illegal business practices by Chinese firms relates to violations of intellectual property rights. African nations do not have the institutions to keep counterfeit and harmful products from entering their territory.[166] Some Chinese manufacturers illicitly copy African designs, such as wax print textiles, and then produce them more cheaply for export back to Africa.[167] These illegal products not only create economic losses for their patent holders, but they also threaten human health and safety. Affecting U.S. companies as well as those of other nationals, counterfeit Chinese goods have flooded the African markets, not only undercutting those who have created the original products and driving them out of the market, but also creating health risks with counterfeit medicines and false products—with Africans once again the victims of this exploitation.

Even more problematic in the longer term is the conduct of Chinese small and medium enterprises, some of which deliberately flout labor and environmental standards as well as local regulations in pursuit of profit.[168] Unscrupulous Chinese traders use front companies to export illegally, everything from timber, diamonds, and prized body parts of endangered wildlife back to China. Chinese triads (criminal gangs) from Hong Kong have moved into Africa as well. Triads have been implicated in the stripping of the southern African coast of abalone (90 percent of which is gone after only a few years), in the shark fin and rhino horn trade, as well as in people trafficking. Seven major triad-affiliated groups, four from Hong Kong and three from Taiwan, have used front companies to engage in illicit trade in wildlife products.

OFFICIAL CHINA RECOGNIZES DAMAGE IN AFRICA CAUSED BY POOR CORPORATE CITIZENS

At the 2006 FOCAC meeting, the Chinese leadership, recognizing that its firms in Africa were not complying with best business practices regarding corruption and environmental degradation, pledged that these firms would be encouraged to behave in an open, fair, just, and transparent way in the future. By 2007, China had issued "good corporate citizen guidelines" to help moderate the conduct of Chinese corporations in Africa.[169] That same year, the World Bank's International Finance Corporation (IFC) and China EXIM Bank signed a memorandum of understanding to work together to publicize and train Chinese banks on the Equator Principles, a voluntary set of social and environmental principles agreed to in 2002. There is evidence that the Chinese MNCs are, as part of the desire to emulate established global MNCs, in the process of embracing aspects of the corporate responsibility agenda.

Beijing's promises to ameliorate the worst behavior of Chinese companies abroad also reflect changing attitudes within China itself, such as calls for a "greener China." In 2008, China EXIM Bank published new guidelines for social and environmental impact assessments.[170] Also in 2007, China's State Forestry Administration and the Ministry of Commerce released guidelines that Chinese logging companies are expected to use abroad. There were no sanctions for not following the logging guidelines, however, and thus, it is not surprising that there continue to be concerns about China's purchase of timber from the African black market (as well as the illegal purchase of African ivory), according to the May 2011 testimony before Congress by George Washington University Professor David Shinn.[171]

As Chinese business has become more deeply embedded in Africa, however, their concerns have shifted from attaining access to resources and market share to sustaining their position and investments.

This can be seen, for example, in the changing attitude of Chinese mining sector companies in Zambia, which have increasingly sought to bring their business practices in line with established legal requirements, such as allowing trade union activity as a safeguard against popular dissent.[172]

AFRICAN CIVIL SOCIETY ACTS TO CONSTRAIN POOR CHINESE BEHAVIOR, BUT MUZZLED CHINESE CIVIL SOCIETY CANNOT LOBBY BEIJING FOR CHANGE

As African civil society—from labor activists and trade analysts to environmental and human rights lobbyists—has developed a voice on the range and breadth of Chinese involvement in continental affairs, civil society actors have also begun to set parameters for Chinese action in collusion with African elites.[173] China's relations with strong, independent African labor unions are not cordial, with labor standards in China sometimes less stringent than in some African countries.[174]

At the same time, there are important actors in the PRC who are missing from the Africa equation: China's civil society. If China's autocratic leaders allowed a free and vibrant civil society, nongovernmental organizations (NGOs), religious groups, etc., might play an important role in curbing the worst Chinese business practices in Africa. Compared to the West and even Japan, societal interest groups figure much less as a factor in shaping China's aid. For example, in the West, NGOs like Oxfam, Save the Children, and Bread for the World lobby parliaments to add funds to the aid budgets reflecting their particular concerns.[175] In China, private and semi-private commercial interests are growing factors in the determination of Chinese assistance, particularly at the provincial levels. China does have an emerging civil society that might also play an influential role were it not severely constrained by the Communist Party. However, China state interests—political, commercial, and bureaucratic—motivated largely by profit, overwhelm the humanitarian civil society influences on aid, and even the independent indigenous blogosphere tends to oppose foreign aid as a waste.

THE CHINESE DIASPORA: LATEST LARGE WAVE IMPACTING AFRICA

Another issue that African governments have yet to grapple with is the impact of Chinese immigration into Africa. Conservative estimates suggest that there are now a million Chinese migrants across the continent.[176] With aid projects at one time or another in every country in Africa but Swaziland and teams of Chinese laborers imported to work on these projects, some stayed behind. This trend accelerated after emigration rules were somewhat relaxed in China in 1985. Once Chinese workers have spent time in African countries, there is a marked tendency for some to stay on, either working on new projects with the Chinese firm that brought them to the continent or branching off into their own small-business pursuits. Thus, the development of Chinese small and medium enterprises in Africa is also tied to the phenomenon of growing Chinese migration to Africa, which is bringing new settler communities to parts of the continent.

The relative scale of Chinese immigration to Africa is also significant. More Chinese have come to Africa in the past 10 years than Europeans have in the past 400,

The Economist claimed in April 2011. Already there are more Chinese living in Nigeria than there were Britons during the height of the Empire, another scholar wrote.[177] Nigerian traders who had shifted their sourcing to China—and who, along with other West Africans, are much in evidence in Guangzhou, Yiwu, and Hong Kong wholesale markets—have felt the shock of competition as Chinese traders have moved directly into Nigeria. Indeed, the opening of three wholesale and retail shopping centers in major urban areas has produced protests from Nigerian businessmen and official action that resulted in their temporary closure.[178] "Across Africa, Chinatowns have sprung up, thousands of Chinese citizens have migrated, with populations now dwarfing white expatriates and traditional Lebanese and Greek networks in many African cities."[179] In the past two presidential elections in Zambia, China's growing influence—including the large population of its nationals—was a key political issue.

Thousands of Chinese retail trading shops are now strung across much of the continent, selling low-cost and low-value products made in China directly to Africa's rural population. The product of individual entrepreneurship, these shops are generally family owned and staffed and rely upon a supply chain stretching back to Hong Kong and the mainland.[180] In Dar Es Salaam, the commercial capital of Tanzania, Chinese are banned from selling in markets. The Tanzanian government announced that the Chinese were welcome as investors but not as "vendors or shoe-shiners."[181] At the same time, it is important to acknowledge that the rise of Chinese retail traders and low-cost imported goods has meant that many Africans could afford new clothes, shoes, radios, and watches for the first time in the lives. Often, Chinese retailers, far from being a curse, have actually been a catalyst for development.

PART III:

CHINA'S STRATEGIC TIES TO AFRICA: OIL, MINERALS, AND AGRICULTURE

In this section, three strategic sectors in China-Africa relations are examined: oil, minerals, and agriculture.

CHINA AND OIL DIPLOMACY IN AFRICA

China's relentless pursuit of economic development turned the country from a petroleum exporter to an importer by 1993—a significant milestone in its development, and an event that also spurred China to adopt a new foreign policy in 1995 emphasizing greater economic ties with Africa. China is currently the second-largest consumer of oil in the world after the United States, with more than half of its crude oil imported. By 2020, official sources estimate that China will import about 65 percent of its oil, and surpass the United States as the world's largest net oil importer.[182] (In terms of overall energy use from all sources including coal, China surpassed the United States in 2010, according to the International Energy Agency [IEA]; in 2000, its energy consumption was half that of the United States.)[183]

Barclays Capital predicted that China's oil consumption in 2015 would be 13.6 million barrels a day, significantly higher than an IEA estimate of 10.5 million.[184] The IEA had earlier projected that China's demand for oil would increase to 14.2 million barrels per day by 2025, with Chinese oil imports equaling current imports by the United States by 2030. Whether China's oil imports surpass those of the United States in 2020 or 2030, it is clear that Africa's importance to China as a source of energy will only increase over time.

The Chinese government has increasingly looked to Africa as a way to diversify, thus reducing dependence on the less stable Middle East, which, in 2010, still accounted for 47 percent of Chinese oil imports.[185] China has developed a two-pronged strategy toward energy investments in Africa to achieve this goal. First, China has pursued exploration and production deals in smaller, low-visibility countries such as Gabon, Equatorial Guinea, and the DRC. Second, it has gone after the largest oil producers, such as Angola, by offering integrated packages of aid.[186] Another key goal of Chinese oil diplomacy in Africa is to foster the growth of Chinese National Oil Companies (NOCs) as players in the global oil market over the long term.[187] Up to now, Chinese efforts to secure oil equity in Africa have not been impressive, and Chinese oil companies are still minor players.[188] The commercial value of the oil investments in Africa by China's NOCs is just 8 percent of the combined commercial value of the international oil companies' investments in African oil, and are often of a magnitude and quality that do not interest Western corporations. Chinese companies have tended to go places for oil where U.S. and European companies are not present, sometimes because they have withdrawn for political reasons under pressure from the international community, such as Sudan, which has sent 60 percent of its oil production to China.

Nevertheless, Western companies are concerned about the increased presence of Chinese NOCs, and complain that the Chinese enjoy an unfair advantage in that their government can link oil investments to government-to-government financial or development assistance, as it did with Angola in 2004.[189] In Niger, for example, the China-Africa Development Fund (CADF) is underwriting a 2000-km pipeline to export oil from the landlocked country that would connect either to Benin or Chad.[190] China is also exploring building an oil refinery in Chad.

Other countries in Africa where China has or is investing in the oil or gas production or exploration include Nigeria, Equatorial Guinea (about 12 percent of its oil exports go to China), Chad, Liberia, and, most recently, Tanzania, where the Chinese government recently signed an agreement to lend $1.06 billion to construct a natural gas pipeline connecting the south of the country to Dar es Salaam.[191] A Chinese company is building Chad's first petroleum refinery in a 60:40 joint venture.[192]

In 2009, China's top three sources of oil in the world were Saudi Arabia, Angola, and Iran, while its top three sources of oil in Africa were Angola, Sudan, and the DRC. Of China's oil imports, 30 percent were sourced from the continent, principally Angola (15.8 percent) and Sudan (6 percent). Recently, Africa's share of China's oil imports increased to about one-third. By contrast, the United States now receives 18-19 percent of its petroleum imports from Africa. In 2009, oil and gas accounted for 64 percent of all African exports to China, and for 90 percent of African exports to the United States. China's oil imports constitute about 13 percent of total African oil exports. The United States and Europe each purchase about one-third of Africa's total oil exports.[193]

China's strategy of using Africa to move away from the Middle East through diversification has not been without risks. Libya had accounted for 3.1 percent of Chinese imports in 2009, but, with Chinese oil imports from Libya disrupted by civil war and the NATO intervention in March 2011, the DRC took third place, and now sends about 50 percent of its production to China.[194] With the independence of South Sudan in July 2011, this new country became China's second most important source of oil. However, when a dispute between Sudan and South Sudan over oil export transport fees broke out, there was a shutoff in oil exports in November 2011. Reflecting the importance of Sudan and South Sudan for Chinese energy imports, Beijing dispatched its special envoy for African Affairs to Khartoum and Juba in December 2011 to propose a solution to the dispute,[195] and dispatched a new envoy in early May 2012 in a renewed diplomatic effort.[196] On May 2, 2012, China joined other UN Security Council members in unanimously supporting Resolution 2046, which called on Sudan and South Sudan to halt cross-border attacks and return to negotiations.

This Sudan example also provides clear evidence of the important oil diplomacy role that the Chinese government can play in African countries. In June 2008 congressional testimony, the Deputy Assistant Secretaries of State for Africa and East Asia noted,

> There are often exaggerated charges that Chinese firms' activities or investment decisions are coordinated by the Chinese government as some sort of strategic gambit in the high-stakes game of global energy security. In reality, Chinese firms compete for profitable projects not only with more technically and politically savvy international firms, but also with each other.[197]

But this testimony missed the point that, while the Chinese government may not have been directing Chinese NOC decisions on which deals to pursue, it has been a strong advocate on behalf of its national oil companies in helping them win deals in Africa.

The Chinese argue that their investment in upstream oil exploration and production in Africa should not be considered threatening, but instead welcomed, since it expands global supplies. It is important to recognize that China frequently chooses not to ship African equity oil back to China. Logistically, it is easier to ship West African oil to markets in Europe and North America. Commercially, the incentive is to choose those markets that fetch the best price. Given its lack of success in securing oil equity in Africa, China, like the United States, will continue to rely overwhelmingly on the open market for years to come.[198] At the same time, Chinese NOCs are becoming more experienced and technologically advanced, including facility in offshore exploration and drilling. Over time, their competitiveness vis-à-vis Western majors will increase in Africa and elsewhere.

CHINA'S STRATEGIC TRADE IN METALS AND MINERALS IN AFRICA — IMPLICATIONS FOR THE UNITED STATES

Access to oil, minerals, and other natural resources has been cited by observers as a core interest of China in Africa, and usually appears as number one of Beijing's top interests in the continent. Much as China has shown a preference for equity oil in developing oil resources in Africa and elsewhere, Beijing also prefers equity minerals and metals. The United States also considers access to African resources one of its core interest in Africa, although this is arguably a lower priority for Washington. The United States imports relatively modest quantities of African mineral products, while China imports huge quantities of cobalt, manganese, tantalum, copper, iron ore, and other minerals.[199]

The case has been made that there is no zero-sum game with the United States in China's massive purchases of African minerals and metals, but rather that these purchases have merely pushed up commodity prices and benefited the continent through friendly competition. Other observers, however, are less sanguine. They note that one worrisome phenomenon in recent years has been Chinese control of the production of more than 90 percent of rare earth minerals. Recently, Chinese companies withheld rare earth minerals from Japan over the Senkaku/Diaoyu Islands dispute and threatened to withhold them from the United States over arms sales to Taiwan. Given China's hostile behavior with rare earth metals, its behavior and intent in terms of securing global supplies of other strategic minerals are valid security issues worth examining. These metals and minerals are important because they are used in key components in communications devices, satellites, and electric fuel cells.

Southern Africa contains several strategic minerals which the United States and its allies require for industrial and military needs. The U.S. Government is particularly concerned about access to critical defense minerals—especially, platinum group metals (PGMs), chromium, and manganese, as well as the rare earth minerals cobalt and uranium—which U.S. arms manufacturers must have access to in order to produce weapons systems. Africa holds 95 percent of the world's reserves of platinum group metals, and 90 percent of its chromite ore reserves.[200] Concerns about China's possibly aggressive and sometimes monopolistic behavior in pursuit of minerals are most acute in three Southern African countries—South Africa, the DRC, and Zambia (with Zimbabwe also being a "country to watch").

South Africa.

Chinese companies have been actively attempting to secure a higher fraction of the world's supply for a number of strategic minerals, particularly manganese ore, chromium, and ferroalloys. In recent years, China has been investing in South Africa's mineral sector, aiming to secure supply of specific commodities for which it has a shortage of reserves. There are reports of an offtake agreement for most of South Africa's annual manganese ore production that has been negotiated by the China Yunnan Metallurgical Company (CYMCO). Over the last 6 years, China has also become involved in South African ferrochrome mining and processing. Chinese companies Sinosteel, Minmetals, and Jiuquan Iron & Steel (Jisco) hold a significant share of various South African ferrochrome producers and explorers. Sinosteel acquired 50 percent of the Tweefontein chrome mine and the Tubatse ferrochrome smelter for a reported $230 million in 2006, creating a joint venture with Samancor known as Tubatse Chrome. Sinosteel also owns 60 percent of Asa Metals, which in turn owns 100 percent of the nearby Dilokong chrome mine. China Minmetals subsidiary, National Minerals, has bought the exploration rights for the Naboom chrome project in the Limpopo province from Mission Point and Versatex for $6.5 million. Jisco is involved in South African mining as a result of a $30 million purchase of 26.1 percent of International Ferro Metals (IFM), which in turn owns the Buffelsfontein chromite mine and smelter. China Metallurgical Group also announced, in late-2011, plans to build an iron-titanium mine in South Africa.[201]

Democratic Republic of the Congo (DRC) and Zambia.

During the Cold War, a core interest of the DRC (then Zaire) for the United States was its role as a secure supplier of cobalt, which is used in aeronautics. Today, 90 percent of China's imported cobalt comes from the DRC (Katanga Province) and Zambia. The 2008 "Sicomines" deal between China and the DRC was a concession to extract 10.6 million tons of copper and 626,619 tons of cobalt, which represented a $9 billion Chinese investment. As part of the Sicomines deal, China is building a road network stretching 4,000 kilometers (2,400 miles) and a railway system spanning 3,200 kilometers (1,920 miles). Three major Chinese companies have a controlling interest of 68 percent in Sicomines. The Congolese company Gecamines has a 32 percent interest. The DRC produces a wide range of other strategic minerals, including uranium, coltan (columbite and tantalum), tungsten, tin, and rare earth minerals. U.S. legislation restricts American companies from operating in the war-torn east of the DRC where strategic minerals for cell-phones (coltan) and electronics are produced.[202]

Future Access: Mitigate Risk through Selective Stockpiling and Encouraging Processing in Southern Africa.

The U.S. Defense Logistics Agency (DLA) is responsible for maintaining the National Defense Stockpile of strategic and critical materials, including base metals such as cobalt and chromium and more precious metals such as platinum, palladium, and iridium. After the Cold War, Congress directed the

DLA to sell the bulk of its stockpiled commodities. With the winding down of wars in Afghanistan and Iraq, and the U.S. Government's strategic pivot back to Asia (read: China), the Defense Department will likely monitor more closely actions by Chinese firms to gain equity stakes in southern African producers of strategic minerals and metals, and may decide, over the longer term, to bolster its stockpiles selectively. One measure that could mitigate any move by China to restrict the free trade in strategic minerals and metals would be to assist Pretoria in developing greater value chains through local processing. At present, China prefers the post-mining processes to take place in China, though some Chinese companies have demonstrated a willingness to engage in such beneficiation overseas through the acquisition or establishment of local production facilities.[203]

CHINA, AFRICA, AND AGRICULTURE: FOOD AS THE NEXT STRATEGIC ASSET?

Guaranteeing agricultural supplies is a matter of national security for the Chinese government. Food makes up more than one-third of the average consumer basket. In 2007, food prices became a key concern, even considered a risk. On several occasions, China's leaders have signaled their concern over the potential risk of higher prices stoking public unrest. China became a net food importer in 2003 – 10 years after it became a net importer of oil. Some observers point to the inevitability of urbanization and the shrinkage of arable land to make the case that China will need to import far more food, and that some of it will increasingly be from Africa. Rising incomes and urbanization are, indeed, leading to dramatic increases in expenditures on food in China. China now has the second highest expenditures on food in the world, behind the United States; by 2015, China's total annual food expenditures will reach over $1 trillion. It has been predicted that China's import demand for agricultural products will grow at double-digit rates over the next 25 years.[204]

Domestically, Beijing is responding by boosting domestic sources of supply, and by attempting to minimize the loss of agricultural land. To ensure food security, China set a red line in 2006 to guarantee that its arable land never shrinks to less than 1.8 billion mu (120 million hectares).[205] However, rapid urbanization and huge investments in railway, highways, and roads in recent years required conversion of agricultural land for other purposes. The province-like municipality of Chongqing has carried out innovative land auctions to convert agricultural to urban land for developers, often with a requirement to "reclaim" nonagricultural land so as to ensure no loss in total arable venues.

Internationally, China is enhancing trade ties to traditional food-exporting nations. Between 2001 and 2010, China's imports of soybeans, for example, rose 10-fold, from $2.8 billion to over $25 billion; 99 percent of China's soybeans come from the Americas. By contrast, China-Africa agricultural trade in 2009 was just $4 billion, less than 4 percent of China's total agricultural trade.[206]

Africa: Potential Source of Agricultural Imports Over Long Term.

Over the long term, Africa has tremendous potential to increase its share of global agricultural exports, most importantly because it has 60 percent of the world's uncultivated, arable land.[207] Already, and starting from a low base, Africa's exports of agricultural products to China have been increasing rapidly. Local specialties such as oranges from Egypt, wine from South Africa, cocoa beans from Ghana, coffee from Uganda, olive oil from Tunisia, and sesame from Ethiopia and Senegal have become familiar to and popular among Chinese consumers.[208]

China is also aligning its aid and investment in African agriculture. China's agricultural engagement with Africa began in the early 1960s as an instrument of diplomacy to counter the agricultural aid program operated by Taiwan. Since then, more than 44 African countries have hosted Chinese agricultural aid projects, and the Chinese have developed more than 90 farms through their aid.[209] Most of these diplomatically useful but unsustainable agricultural projects failed, however. In recent years, the Chinese government shifted toward a strategy encouraging the takeover of these often moribund turnkey projects by China's nascent agribusiness corporations. Examples of takeovers by Chinese companies include a sisal farm privatized by the Tanzanian government, a rice farm in Guinea, a tea plantation in Mali, and sugar complexes in Madagascar and Togo.

In May 2006, 40 domestic and international experts developed a roadmap for China's strategic planners recommending agricultural technology and seed cultivation as two areas in which China could be competitive. The experts also recommended that China establish cutting-edge agricultural technology demonstration parks across Africa, and Beijing now plans to establish 14 such parks. [210]

Today, state-owned agribusiness enterprises carry out many of China's agricultural investments in Africa, some of which are aid projects executed under contract by the Chinese government for the recipient nation. Increasingly, however, these projects are for profit from their inception. The Chinese government, as part of the broader "going-out" policy initiated in 2001, provides PRC companies with a separate set of incentives for agricultural investments.

Up to now, Chinese policy support for outward investment in agriculture, as in other sectors, is focused on large enterprises. At the central level, the most significant national SOE active in this sector is the China State Farm Agribusiness Corporation (CSFAC), which operates in several countries. CSFAC and the Jiangsu Provincial State Farm Agribusiness Corporation (SFAC) established the China-Zambia Friendship Farm, which devotes 667 hectares to growing barley, maize, and soybeans. Six Chinese SOEs had established 15 farms in Zambia with a total of 10,000 hectares as of 2008. At the provincial level, there are also examples of agricultural investments in several African countries, but none are truly large scale. Hubei Province SFAC established a 1,000 hectare demonstration farm in 2005 in Mozambique using a grant of land from the host government; the SFAC subsequently formed Lianfeng Overseas Agricultural Development Co. to expand its activities in Mozambique and other countries in Africa. The Shaanxi SFAS established a 5,000 hectare farm with a $62.5 million investment in Cameroon, mainly growing rice. Another project involves a Chongqing SFAC growing rice in Tanzania. [211]

In May 2008, press reports claiming that China's Ministry of Agriculture was in the process of formulating a new policy on outward investment in agriculture attracted international concern about Chinese "land grabs." The Director General of the UN's Food and Agricultural Organization (FAO), obliquely referring to countries including China, said in August 2008 that "the race for food-importing countries to secure farmland overseas to improve their food security risks creating a neo-colonial system." Likely in response to international criticism, as well as to local opposition as in Mozambique, China's National Development and Reform Commission (NDRC) announced in November 2008 a 20-year food-security strategy explicitly stating that foreign land acquisitions would not be part of China's strategy.[212] Under China's communist system, all land still belongs to the State, though rural land is owned "collectively." This ideologically driven prohibition in China of private ownership of land suggests that Beijing would have been particularly sensitive to foreign criticism of land grabs in Africa, and that such criticism was likely also a factor in the NDRC decision.

News reports indicated in January 2012 that a company from China's Hainan Province had won Sierra Leone's approval for a $1.23 billion investment in rice and rubber production on 40,000 hectares. If true, this would be a break in the pattern of smaller-scale leases by Chinese firms. However, given the number of articles in the past on Chinese agricultural investments that have subsequently been proven false, such a large figure may be inaccurate.[213] For example, Chinese telecom multinational ZTE reportedly had signed a joint venture in 2007 to produce oil palm biofuels using 3 million hectares in the DRC; the DRC government subsequently indicated it had approved only 100,000 hectares, and the project's future is still uncertain.[214]

Conclusion: Reports of Chinese Land Grabs in Africa Exaggerated

Reports of Chinese land grabs in Africa are over-stated. Arab states, including Libya, Egypt, Jordan, Kuwait, Qatar, the United Arab Emirates, and Saudi Arabia—as well as private investors from throughout the developing and developed world—have indeed made recent land acquisitions in Africa. By contrast, Beijing, alarmed by local criticism, has remained cautious about large land purchases by Chinese companies. Some Chinese businessmen do see Africa as a target for grain-production exports to the Chinese market, and as a source of biofuels. Chinese firms sought deals for biofuel palm oil in the DRC in 2007 and biofuel jatropha in Zambia in 2009.[215] Yet, the Chinese appear to be investing primarily via cooperative projects rather than exclusive land deals.[216] So far, Chinese investment in African farming, forestry, fishing, and animal husbandry has accounted for only 3.1 percent of its FDI.

PART IV:

U.S. RESPONSES TO CHINA IN AFRICA

POTENTIAL FOR U.S.-CHINA COOPERATION IN AFRICA: LIMITED AND CONSTRAINED BY BEIJING

China's foreign policy toward Africa all too often legitimizes human rights abuses and undemocratic practices under the guise of noninterference in the internal affairs of other countries.[217] At a U.S. Senate hearing on China in Africa on November 1, 2011, lawmakers criticized China's state-backed support for governments with poor human rights records, stating that "China is interested in [its] own goals and has very little concern about the governance of the countries that they deal with."

In fact, Beijing selectively welcomes good governance — when it protects the trade and investment interests of Chinese businesses, e.g., in an advanced economy like South Africa. In general, however, China undermines Western goals of promoting democracy, good governance, and human rights in Africa by: 1) enabling certain governments, such as Zimbabwe and Ethiopia, to restrict the flow of information on the Internet;[218] 2) granting aid and trade credits without conditionality related to good governance; and, 3) ignoring when its rent-seeking businessmen use bribery and gifts to win contracts and government approvals.

While Beijing's "no-strings attached" approach to aid appeals to some African elites, it also poses a direct challenge to the good governance focus of the Washington Consensus.[219] The Washington Consensus involved the imposition of conditionalities by the World Bank, IMF, and donors regarding macroeconomic policy, public spending, and transparency as well as, in some cases, the holding of democratic elections by African governments. Chinese involvement in Africa has sparked talk in the West of an emerging Beijing Consensus predicated on noninterference in domestic affairs of states. Ethiopian Prime Minister Meles Zanawi, speaking at the January 2012 inauguration of the new AU headquarters paid for by China, claimed that the recent rapid growth experienced by many African countries had coincided with a trend toward the adoption of China's state-led economic model. The Prime Minister excoriated *The Economist* — a standard-bearer magazine of the Washington Consensus — for having published a banner headline a decade ago that Africa was "The Hopeless Continent," only to recently publish a new banner headline that simply read "Africa Rising."[220] Sidestepping a journalist's question about whether Africans should follow the Washington or the Beijing Consensus, Chinese Premier Wen Jiabao said at the 2009 FOCAC that "Africa's development should be based on its own conditions and should follow its own path, that is, the African model."[221]

In this context of an authoritarian, nationalistic, and mercantilist China, what real potential is there for cooperation with the United States in Africa? From a pragmatic perspective, there should be some grounds for cooperation. After all, both China and the United States have similar interests in gaining access to Africa's vast energy and raw material resources, and both require a stable geopolitical environment on the continent in order for them to achieve their objectives. For example, China's willingness in May 2012 to work with the United States in the UN Security Council to pass Resolution 2046 on Sudan and South Sudan primarily reflects its desire to see oil exports from the Sudans resumed as soon as possible.

The rhetoric of official U.S. policy has been that there has not been a zero-sum competition with China for influence in Africa. In this view, there is no inherent strategic conflict between China and the United States in Africa: Sino-American cooperation in Africa is not only possible, but it is in the interests of all stakeholders who seek to promote Africa's development and integration into the global economy.[222]

In theory, China and the United States could potentially work together to build the export capacity of African industries; provide technical assistance on climate change; and collaborate on peacekeeping operations, anti-piracy operations, countering drug smuggling, and disaster relief.[223] U.S. Assistant Secretary of State for African Affairs Johnnie Carson, following a November 2011 trip to China, said that, "We are eager to see if we can work with China to leverage our comparative advantages to help Africa overcome some of it economic challenges, particularly in the area of agriculture, health, and clean water."[224]

Moreover, there have already been precedents for U.S.-China cooperation within several African countries. In Liberia, for example, the U.S. Government trained staff and refurbished the Ministry of Defense headquarters. China provided vehicles and computer equipment, and is providing some specialty training and rebuilding at least one base up-country. Good communication between the U.S. and Chinese embassies on the ground in Liberia has helped each party identify areas for inputs.[225] This occurred, for example, where China and the United States agreed to join forces to combat malaria, and collaborated in the construction of the military barracks at Bonga for a UN peacekeeping operation.[226] In agriculture, the U.S. and Chinese Ambassadors in Ethiopia arranged exchanges to observe demonstration farms each country has built to increase agricultural capacity. In Gabon, a U.S. official said recently, the United States hopes to work with China and Gabonese public health experts on preventing the emergence of infectious diseases.[227]

The reality, however, is that Beijing is not really interested in broad-based strategic cooperation with the United States in Africa, so we will continue to have only occasional showcase examples of cooperation instead of true, sustained, and strategic cooperation. One reason is Beijing's fear that coordinated U.S.-China diplomatic engagement could raise suspicions among some African parties that the United States and China are ganging up against them. The major reason, however, is domestic PRC politics, which are marked by hyper-mistrust of the United States. This mistrust reflects a strong nationalism and the Communist Party's strict control of the news media, which can create a nationalistic echo chamber of anti-American propaganda that makes it hard for positive images of the United States to be seen, and even harder for advocates of greater cooperation with the United States to speak up.

Another Chinese sensitivity, particularly for the China's Communist Party, is how any potential cooperation is framed. If contributions from the Chinese side for a joint cooperative project appear to be equal or even superior to those of the American side, then it might be accepted by the Chinese side. However, even a humanitarian project in which the American side's contribution (e.g., visit of a hospital ship) appears to be more impressive than that of the Chinese side (e.g., medical teams supporting a strengthened health care system), it would likely be rejected for reasons of "face" and the need for Chinese propaganda to weed out unfavorable comparisons with foreign partners. In this regard, joint U.S.-China cooperation in the fight against malaria might be promising. The Chinese are particularly proud of the anti-malarial drug Artemsinin, which was based on traditional Chinese medicine, so they might be willing to cooperate in this very narrow area.

The United States is trying to use bilateral diplomacy to shift China's policies in Africa. U.S. Under Secretary of State for Economic Affairs Robert D. Hormats said at a recent meeting of the U.S.-China Strategic and Economic Dialogue that the United States supported Chinese investment and aid to African economies but that, consistent with global norms, Beijing should adopt more transparent financing to combat corruption, and impose stricter environmental and labor standards. China can play a constructive role in Africa as an investor, but needs to be a responsible investor, Hormats said. In a sense, this is an Africa-specific corollary of the U.S. theme, first championed by then Deputy Secretary of State (and former World Bank President) Robert Zoellick, that a rising China should become a responsible stakeholder on the global scene.[228]

Unfortunately, U.S. Government efforts are unlikely to influence China's policies in Africa. In the trade sphere, China uses East Asian mercantilist policies, including currency manipulation and domestic innovation rules discriminating against foreign firms to circumvent its WTO commitments. In general, Beijing's authoritarian government thinks only of China's interests and will resist international pressure. In

November 1, 2011, testimony before the U.S. Senate, American University professor Deborah Brautigam made a suggestion on how to encourage China to become a more responsible stakeholder in Africa:

> The OECD sets the standard for being a responsible global player. . . . The Chinese by and large are familiar with these rules. We need to think about ways in which we can make actually joining the club—as South Korea and Mexico have recently done—both feasible and attractive to the Chinese.

The problem with this suggestion is multifold. First, China is unlikely to agree to have its companies constrained by OECD rules without spending a few more years learning how to "go global," much as it insisted on long phase-in periods for many sectors prior to its WTO accession. When China no longer sees itself as a developing country but rather as an emerging middle-income country, only then will it seriously consider joining the OECD. However, it is not certain China would ever wish to join the OECD, as this could undermine its leadership among non-aligned countries of the south, nor is it certain that other OECD members would accept China as a member of this democrats' club. Worse still, even if China did join the OECD, it would likely pay only lip service to its commitments on aid, trade credits, and anti-bribery. Specifically, China would do the utmost to nullify its commitments by skirting or ignoring the rules, much as it does at present in the WTO.

CONCLUSION:
RECOMMENDATIONS FOR
U.S. POLICYMAKERS

What, then, should U.S. policymakers do in the face of China's rapid rise and advance in Africa, and its minimal interest in collaborating with the United States on the African continent? Here are four recommendations:

1. Face up To China's Commercial Challenge in Africa by Strengthening U.S. Economic Diplomacy. One central argument of this monograph is that national strength and security ultimately depend on a strong economic foundation. In this regard, the United States needs to work proactively to improve its competitive position in Africa vis-à-vis China and other emerging nations. It could do this in a number of ways:

- Biannual Presidential Summits with African Heads of State: Organize a U.S. Presidential summit with African heads of state in Washington in the summer of 2014, and do so biannually again in 2016 and beyond. Historically, AGOA Forums have rotated annually between Washington and an African capital. The next U.S. President, whether a re-elected President Obama or a new Republican President, could travel to the next AGOA Forum in Africa in the summer of 2013 as a part of a multi-country tour of African nations. This could then set the stage for the first-ever U.S. Presidential summit with African heads of state in Washington in the summer of 2014. Strong economic diplomacy begins with building personal relationships, and starting at the top also sends a message to the U.S. Government, Congress, and the American people that Africa is an important market that we, as a nation, will not ignore. Members of the U.S. cabinet, such as the Treasury and Energy Secretary, should also travel more frequently to Africa to the extent that their portfolios allow them to promote U.S. goods and services.

- Boost U.S. Export Promotion in Africa: President Obama's National Export Initiative announced March 11, 2010, and Secretary Clinton's October 14, 2011, speech on economic statecraft were excellent statements of intent, but need to be converted into sustained, multiyear action with real resources behind them. The President sought a 5 percent increase in the fiscal year 2013 budget for the U.S. Department of Commerce — a powerful statement that his administration intends to promote U.S. exports, despite a severely constrained budgetary environment. The Administration and Congress should work in a bipartisan fashion to ensure increased funding for promotion of U.S. exports to Africa, including:
  - (Re)opening USFCS offices in Africa;
  - Increased funding for USTDA, USEXIM Bank, and even OPIC activities in Africa (because U.S. investment abroad often leads to U.S. exports as well); and,
  - Expanded, mandatory commercial training for U.S. State Department Foreign Service Officers (FSOs) serving at U.S. Embassies in Africa with no USFCS presence.

The Administration and Congress should also consider shifting USFCS back into the State Department and, at a minimum, modifying the promotion criteria for State Department FSOs to make successful U.S. export encouragement and enhancement a key factor in selection of Chiefs of Mission and in FSO promotions.

2. Match China's New Soft Power in Africa by Funding U.S. Soft Power. As noted above, another reason for China's newly found success in Africa is its expanded development and use of soft power. Several elements of its soft power diplomacy are lifted from the U.S. diplomatic playbook, including training and scholarships; cultural and language centers; promoting news services; developing a volunteer corps; and an international visitor program. The United States should continue to fund its successful soft power efforts adequately in Africa, including public diplomacy, the Fulbright program, and the Peace Corps. At a time when China has opened many Confucius Centers in Africa, the United States should be opening, not closing, more American Cultural Centers.

3. Review U.S. Policy on Strategic Metals Stockpiling: Seek China's Peaceful Rise, But Prepare for the Worst. In raising strategic metals as an issue, I do not intend to suggest that the United States and China are heading toward an armed conflict at any point in the 21st century or beyond. A central and unwaveringly correct tenet of U.S. foreign policy toward China is to welcome its peaceful rise. At the same time, prudence calls us to revisit U.S. policy on the stockpiling of certain strategic metals. As noted above, Chinese companies—upon instructions from the Chinese government—withheld rare earth minerals from Japan over the Senkaku/Diaoyu Islands dispute and threatened to withhold them from the United States over arms sales to Taiwan. Given that China has already engaged in hostile behavior with rare earth metals, the

United States has every right to be wary of China's intentions, and should monitor more closely actions by Chinese firms to gain equity stakes in southern African producers of strategic minerals and metals. If appropriate, the United States should selectively bolster its strategic stockpiles.

Chinese culture is rich in sayings, including those from Sun Tzu's *Art of War*. At the same time, the West has a few of its own. One of these is the Latin adage "*si vis pacem, para bellum,*" or "if you wish peace, prepare for war."

4. Never Give Up Hope: Is Maritime Security in the Gulf of Guinea One Area of Possible U.S.-China Cooperation? I argued above that the scope for U.S.-China cooperation in Africa is narrow, mainly because of the hyper-mistrust of the U.S. Government by Beijing's Communist Party. This is not to suggest that U.S. policymakers should give up in seeking ways to cooperate with China to the extent that U.S. national interests are served as well. As a Chinese proverb puts it, "Seek common ground while putting aside differences." Given Beijing's wariness about cooperation, one pragmatic way to do this in Africa is to take our cue from areas in which Beijing has stated that international action is needed.

One example of an area in which such bilateral cooperation in Africa may be possible is in helping countries in West and Central Africa to better control their maritime domain. In this regard, Chinese Deputy Permanent Representative to the United Nations Wang Min called on the international community on October 19, 2011, to provide assistance actively in combating piracy in the Gulf of Guinea:

> The coastal countries [of West and Central Africa] and the international community need to attach great importance to the root cause of piracy in the Gulf of Guinea, adopt comprehensive strategies, [and] strengthen security capacity building.[229]

As the section above on oil diplomacy suggests, there is a commonality of interests for the United States and China in ensuring safe shipping routes and uninterrupted oil production in the Gulf of Guinea, whose offshore oil reserves are already the largest in the world. The problem of illicit activities in the maritime domain of littoral states of the Gulf of Guinea is serious and worsening, fundamentally threatening the region's stability and development. Besides piracy, these illicit activities include trafficking in drugs, arms, and people; illegal fishing; and dumping of waste.

China has already shown its willingness to contribute to the fight against piracy in East Africa. Therefore, an important precedent for international cooperation has already been established within China's foreign policy and military communities for anti-piracy cooperation in the Gulf of Guinea. Wang made his comments on the same day as an open debate in the UN Security Council on the topic of "Peace and Security in Africa: Piracy in the Gulf of Guinea," convened by Nigeria in its capacity as rotating monthly President of the Security Council. Nigeria convened this debate at the request of Benin and other countries in the region. UN Secretary General Ban Ki-moon, in a January 18 letter to the Security Council, recalled the October Security Council debate, noted how China had agreed to fund the purchase of a ship for Benin, and called on all international partners to:

provide logistical support to ECOWAS and ECCAS to improve their capabilities to counter piracy . . . in particular with regard to infrastructure, radar, communications equipment and training of maritime security personnel.[230]

Therefore, there is existing strong African and UN support for collective international action to counter piracy (and other illicit activities) in the Gulf of Guinea. Under the cover of the UN Secretary General's call for action, and at the urging of several countries in West and Central Africa, including Nigeria and Benin, China may be willing to explore with the United States how the two could collaborate with other nations to fight piracy and other illicit activities in the Gulf of Guinea.

Given the radically different nature of illicit activities in the Gulf of Guinea, the focus of coordination and burden sharing by the United States and China could be on training and equipping West and Central African navies and coast guards—not on patrols by the international community itself. West and Central Africa, unlike East Africa, do not face the problem of a failed state with a long coastline—Somalia. They have not ceded their sovereignty and would not welcome prolonged patrols by the international community in their territorial waters or Exclusive Economic Zones (EEZs). The United States, for its part, may also be very leery of seeing Chinese naval vessels entering the south Atlantic, even if they would be a great distance from the U.S. homeland. To address our own concerns, we could continue the positive work with African navies via the Africa Partnership Station (APS) and the African Maritime Law Enforcement Program (AMLEP) programs—which include the use of U.S.

naval and coast guard vessels—while encouraging China to focus on equipping African naval and coast guards toward a primarily law-enforcement mission in the Gulf of Guinea, not on patrolling or training aboard Chinese vessels.

ENDNOTES

1. A "supercycle" is a prolonged-trend (decade or more) rise in real commodity prices.

2. The four countries are Burkina Faso, Swaziland, Gambia, and São Tomé and Principe.

3. Harry Verhoeven, "Africa Looks East," Oxford University China Africa Network, February 12, 2011, p. 1.

4. "Lions on the Move: the Progress and Potential of African Economies," McKinsey Global Institute, June 2010.

5. David H. Shinn, "China's Growing Role in Africa: Implications for U.S. Policy," testimony before Senate Committee on Foreign Relations Subcommittee on African Affairs, November 1, 2011.

6. *Ibid.*

7. Robert I. Rotberg, ed., "China into Africa—Trade, Aid, and Influence," Washington, DC: The Brookings Institution, 2008, p. 297.

8. Chris Alden, "China in Africa," London, UK: International African Institute/Royal African Society/Social Science Research Council, 2007, p. 35.

9. David H. Shinn, "The Impact of China's Growing Influence in Africa," *The European Financial Review*, April-May 2011.

10. Rotberg, p. 65.

11. Matthew Plowright, "China & Africa: Law of the Land," September 6, 2011, available from *www.emergingmarkets.org*.

12. "Regional Economic Outlook—Sub-Saharan Africa—Sustaining the Expansion," Washington, DC: International Monetary Fund, October 2011, pp. 2, 39-41.

13. "China, Africa, and the World Bank: Partners in a Journey of Discovery," Washington, DC: The World Bank Group, October 8, 2010.

14. Assanatou Balde, "India-Africa Summit: A New Economic Meeting," *Frontier Advisory*, May 24, 2011, available from *Afrik. com*.

15. Nayanima Basu, "India-Africa Trade to Reach $70 billion by 2015," May 19, 2011, available from *rediff.com*.

16. Shinn, "China's Growing Role in Africa."

17. Louise Redvers, "India Steps Up Scramble with China for African Energy," *Pambazuka News*, February 4, 2010.

18. David Lewis, "Special Report: In Africa, can Brazil be the anti-China?" Reuters, February 23, 2011.

19. Ed Cropley, "Scramble for Africa: Brazil Gaining Ground on China," *Pambazuka News*, November 5, 2009.

20. Fabiola Ortiz, "Brazil Forging Strategic Alliance with Africa," Interpress Service (IPS), May 7, 2012.

21. *Ibid.*

22. Lewis.

23. Alexander Gabuev, "Russia in Africa: An Alternative to China's Investment Monopoly?" *Kommersant*, December 20, 2011.

24. Andew Batson, "Africa, China and Getting Beyond Resources," *The Wall Street Journal*, September 13, 2010.

25. Shinn, "China's Growing Role in Africa."

26. *McKinsey Global Institute Quarterly*, 2010.

27. Charles Robertson and Lucy Corkin, "China in Africa," *Renaissance Capital*, April 21, 2011.

28. *VOANews.com*, quoting National Committee of the Chinese People's Political Consultative Conference (CPPCC) Chairman Jia Qinlin at AU headquarters inauguration, January 28, 2012.

29. Shinn, "The Impact of China's Growing Influence in Africa"; see also "Sino-Africa Trade and Financial Cooperation: History and Trends," Bank of China, May 2011.

30. Source: U.S. Department of Commerce, available from *www.census.gov/foreign-trade/balance/c0013.html*.

31. Bank of China.

32. David H. Shinn, "The Role of China in Africa: Trade, Investment and Aid," Social Investment Forum International Working Group, Spring Symposium, May 18, 2010.

33. Bank of China.

34. A tariff line is the product code used at the national level, beyond the six digits of the Harmonized Commodity Description and Coding System (HS) developed by the World Customs Organization (WCO). China has 7,550 8-digit tariff lines per the China-Pakistan Free Trade Agreement. This suggests that China is making tariff concessions to Africa on over 62 percent of its tariff lines.

35. *Ibid.*

36. Robertson.

37. Bank of China.

38. "Regional Economic Outlook—Sub-Saharan Africa—Sustaining the Expansion," International Monetary Fund, October 2011, pp. 39, 48.

39. Deborah Brautigam, "The Dragon's Gift: The Real Story of China in Africa," Oxford, 2009.

40. Shinn, "China's Growing Role in Africa."

41. "Regional Economic Outlook—Sub-Saharan Africa—Sustaining the Expansion," Washington, DC: International Monetary Fund, October 2011, p. 48.

42. Robertson.

43. Mthuli Ncube *et al.*, "Chinese Trade and Investment Activities in Africa," African Development Bank, Policy Brief, Vol. 1, Issue 4, July 29, 2010, p. 7.

44. "China Becomes South Africa's Biggest Export Destination: Ambassador," *Xinhua*, August, 21, 2011.

45. Hayley Herman *et al.*, "South-South Relations: Sino-African Engagement and Cooperation," Emerging Powers in Africa Programme, Cape Town, South Africa: July 21, 2010.

46. Shinn, "The Role of China in Africa."

47. Harry Verhoeven and Nikia Clarke, "OUCAN Conference Report: 'Chinese Investment and African Agency,' Main Conclusions," Oxford University China Africa Network, April 7, 2011.

48. Taylor, p. 14.

49. "Into Africa—Institutional Investor Intentions to 2016," Invest AD/Economist Intelligence Unit, January 2012, p. 7.

50. Mutsu Chironga *et al.*, "The Globe: Cracking the Next Growth Market: Africa," *Harvard Business Review*, May 2011.

51. *Ibid.*

52. "Regional Economic Outlook—Sub-Saharan Africa—Sustaining Growth Amid Global Uncertainty," International Monetary Fund, April 2012, p. 4.

53. "It's Time for Africa": Ernst & Young's 2011 Africa Attractiveness Survey, Ernst & Young, 2011, p. 35.

54. Available from *www.princeton.edu/~pcwcr/reports/benin 1990.html*.

55. "Into Africa," p. 9.

56. *Ibid.*, pp. 7-8.

57. *Ibid.*, p. 18.

58. "Lions on the Move: The Progress and Potential of African Economies," McKinsey Global Institute, June 2010.

59. "It's Time for Africa," Ernst & Young, p. 3.

60. J. Peter Pham, "Assessing China's Role and Influence in Africa," testimony before U.S. House of Representatives Subcommittee on Africa, Global Health, and Human Rights, March 29, 2012, p. 3.

61. "Into Africa," p. 7.

62. *Ibid.*, pp. 7, 15.

63. "Lions on the Move."

64. *Harvard Business Review.*

65. Rotberg, p. 51.

66. Brautigam, "The Dragon's Gift," pp. 80, 82-83.

67. Alden, p. 114.

68. Brautigam, "The Dragon's Gift," p. 78.

69. "China's Mighty Telecom Footprint in Africa," The New Security Foundation, February 14, 2011.

70. Pham, March 29, 2012, p. 6.

71. Alden, p. 102.

72. Peter Wonacott, "In Africa, U.S. Watches China's Rise," *The Wall Street Journal*, September 2, 2011.

73. Verhoeven, p. 1.

74. Martyn Davies, "How China Is Influencing Africa's Development," OECD Development Centre, Background Paper, April 2010, p. 6.

75. Anonymous East African Minister, Africa Center for Strategic Studies' "African Executive Dialogue" meeting, November 2011, Washington, DC.

76. Alden, p. 132.

77. Verhoeven, p. 1.

78. Raymond Hu, "Chinese Investment in Africa: A Dangerous Game," *American Foreign Policy*, Princeton Student Editorials on Global Politics, March 16, 2011.

79. Taylor, p. 24.

80. Shinn, "China's Growing Role in Africa."

81. Stephen Hayes, President, Corporate Council on Africa, "Assessing China's Role and Influence in Africa," testimony before U.S. House of Representatives Subcommittee on Africa, Global Health, and Human Rights, March 29, 2012, p .3.

82. Yun Sun, Visiting Fellow at the Brookings Institution's Northeast Asia Policy Studies, in public remarks, "The Dragon and the Eagle" conference on China and the United States in Africa, Virginia Military Institute, Lexington, VA, November 3-4, 2011.

83. Shinn, "China's Growing Role in Africa."

84. Alden, p. 14.

85. "White Paper on China-Africa Economic and Trade Cooperation," People's Republic of China (PRC) Information Office of the State Council, December 1, 2010.

86. Xie Yajing, "China-Africa Trade Is Witnessing New Development Opportunities," *ChinAfrica*, January 18, 2011.

87. Alden, p. 23.

88. Overseas commercial programs were transferred from the Department of State to the Department of Commerce under the "Trade Agreements Act of 1979." See *Foreign Service Journal*, April 2005, p. 20.

89. Websites of U.S. Commercial Service, China Ministry of Commerce (MOFCOM) as of February 7, 2012.

90. Jennifer G. Cooke, "China's Soft Power in Africa," from Chap. 3 of "Chinese Soft Power and its Implications for the United States," Washington, DC: Center for Strategic and International Studies (CSIS), March 10, 2009; Taylor, p. 24.

91. Shinn, "China's Growing Role in Africa."

92. U.S. Principal Deputy Assistant Secretary of State for Africa Don Yamamoto, "Assessing China's Role and Influence in Africa," testimony before U.S. House of Representatives Subcommittee on Africa, Global Health, and Human Rights, March 29, 2012.

93. "Zaoan Feizhou (Good Morning, Africa!)," *Jeune Afrique*, February 12-18, 2012.

94. Alden, p. 27.

95. Testimony by U.S. Deputy Assistant Secretary of State James Swan, Bureau of African Affairs, before U.S. Senate Foreign Relations Subcommittee on African Affairs, June 4, 2008.

96. Brautigam, "The Dragon's Gift."

97. Shinn, "China's Growing Role in Africa."

98. Brautigam, "The Dragon's Gift."

99. Robertson.

100. Brautigam, "The Dragon's Gift," pp. 291, 299.

101. *Ibid.*

102. "White Paper on China-Africa Economic and Trade Co-operation," People's Republic of China (PRC) Information Office of the State Council, December 1, 2010.

103. Herman.

104. Taylor, p. 22.

105. Brautigam, "The Dragon's Gift."

106. "U.S. 'losing' sway in Africa as China rises," November 2, 2011, available from *www.news24.com/Africa/News/US-losing-sway-in-Africa-as-China-rises-20111102.*

107. "White Paper on China-Africa Economic and Trade Co-operation," People's Republic of China (PRC) Information Office of the State Council, December 1, 2010.

108. Shinn, "China's Growing Role in Africa."

109. Sanusha Naidu, "Africa Becoming Low Cost Manufacturing Hub for Chinese Investments," *Pambazuka News,* May 27, 2010.

110. Deborah Brautigam, testimony on China's Growing Role in Africa, U.S. Senate Committee on Foreign Relations Subcommittee on African Affairs, November 1, 2011.

111. Richard Behar, "China Storms Africa," *Fast Company,* June 1, 2008.

112. "China International Fund—The Queensway Syndicate and the Africa Trade," *The Economist*, August 13, 2011; Lee Levkovitz *et al.*, "The 88 Queensway Group—A Case Study of Chinese Investors' Operations in Angola and Abroad," U.S.-China Economic & Security Review Commission.

113. "Guinea: Blood and Money In the Streets," *Pambazuka News*, October 22, 2009.

114. Verhoeven, p. 1.

115. Rotberg, p. 18.

116. Alden, p. 124.

117. "Zambian Investors Say Copper Boom to Continue as Sata Says It's No Castro," *Bloomberg*, Oct 20, 2011.

118. Brautigam, testimony on China's Growing Role in Africa.

119. Rotberg, p. 9.

120. Swan, 2008.

121. PRC Premier Wen Jiabao, "Speech: "Building the New Type of China-Africa Strategic Partnership," *Pambazuka News*, November 12, 2009.

122. Davies, pp. 14, 17.

123. J. Stephen Morrison, "Testimony Before the U.S. Senate Committee on Foreign Relations Subcommittee on African Affairs," June 4, 2008, Washington, DC: Center for Strategic and International Studies.

124. Robinson.

125. Plowright.

126. Robertson.

127. Brautigam, testimony on China's Growing Role in Africa.

128. Brautigam, "The Dragon's Gift."

129. Rotberg, p. 119.

130. Alden, p. 113.

131. *McKinsey Quarterly*, 2010.

132. Peter Wonacott, "Small Factories Take Root in Africa," *The Wall Street Journal*, September 24, 2011.

133. Robertson.

134. Brautigam, "The Dragon's Gift," p. 188.

135. "Kenya: Local Factory to Assemble Chinese Vehicles," August 10, 2011, available from *allAfrica.com*.

136. "The Chinese in Africa — Trying to Pull Together — Africans Are Asking Whether China Is Making Their Lunch or Eating It," *The Economist*, April 20, 2011.

137. Brautigam, "The Dragon's Gift," pp. 223-224.

138. Rotberg, p. 112.

139. Brautigam, "The Dragon's Gift," p. 211.

140. *Ibid.*, pp. 89, 91, 192, 194.

141. Rotberg, p. 106.

142. Taylor, pp. 71, 73, 77.

143. Raphael Kaplinski, "What Does the Rise of China Do for Industrialization in Sub-Saharan Africa?" *Review of African Political Economy*, Vol. 35, No. 115, 2008, pp. 7-22.

144. Rotberg, p. 70.

145. Brautigam, "The Dragon's Gift,"pp. 198-199.

146. *Ibid.*, p. 91.

147. Deborah Brautigam and Tang Xiaoyang, "African Shenzhen: China's Special Economic Zones in Africa," *Journal of Modern African Studies*, Vol. 49, No. 1, 2011, pp. 27-54.

148. Davies, p. 24.

149. Taylor, p. 84.

150. Rotberg, p. 141.

151. Brautigam, "The Dragon's Gift," p. 101.

152. Deborah Brautigam and Tang Xiaoyang, "China's Investment in African Special Economic Zones: Overview and Initial Lessons," The World Bank, draft, December 2009, pp. 10-11, 17.

153. "Chinese Investment Energizes Zambia's Development," *Xinhua*, August 19, 2011.

154. Thomas Farole, Deborah Brautigam, and Tang Xiaoyang, "China's Investment in Special Economic Zones: Prospects, Challenges, and Opportunities," The World Bank – Economic Premise, March 2010, Number 5, p. 4.

155. Brautigam, "The Dragon's Gift," p. 97.

156. Qiang Lijing and Tan Zhe, "Chinese Investment Buoys Africa's Economy," *Xinhua*, September 9, 2011.

157. Brautigam and Tang, "China's Investment in African Special Economic Zones."

158. Albert N. Link and John T. Scott, "The Growth of the Research Triangle Park," Nottingham, UK: University of Nottingham, September 18-19, 2000, p. 4.

159. "Tunis Conference Puts Sino-Africa Trade Ties Under Microscope," *Pambazuka News*, January 21, 2010.

160. Taylor, p. 161.

161. Chris Alden, "Paving the Way for the Next Stage in China-African Relations," *Pambazuka News*, November 26, 2009.

162. "Regional Economic Outlook—Sub-Saharan Africa—Sustaining the Expansion," Washington, DC: International Monetary Fund, October 2011, p. 53.

163. Ncube, July 29, 2010, p. 2.

164. *The Economist*, April 20, 2011.

165. Brautigam, "The Dragon's Gift."

166. Shinn, "China's Growing Role in Africa."

167. Taylor, p. 77.

168. Alden, pp. 14, 58, 88.

169. Rotberg, p. 13.

170. Brautigam, "China's Gift," pp. 301, 303.

171. Shinn, "China's Growing Role in Africa."

172. Alden, pp. 4, 56, 90, 116, 121.

173. Alden, pp. 37, 60, 84.

174. Shinn, "China's Growing Role in Africa."

175. Brautigam, "The Dragon's Gift," pp. 15, 16, 86.

176. Leo Lewis, "China's Africa Ambitions Threaten Policy," *The Australian*, October 17, 2011.

177. Behar.

178. Alden, p. 48.

179. Verhoeven, p. 1.

180. Alden, pp. 4, 14.

181. *The Economist*, April 20, 2011.

182. Christopher Alesi and Stephanie Hanson, "Expanding China-Africa Oil Ties," New York: Council on Foreign Relations, February 8, 2012.

183. Shelly Zhao, "The Geopolitics of China-African Oil," China Briefing, April 13, 2011.

184. Chua Baizhen, "China's Oil Demand to Surpass IEA Forecasts, Barclays Says," *Bloomberg*, November 23, 2011.

185. Alessi.

186. Stephanie Hanson, "China, Africa, and Oil," New York: Council on Foreign Relations, June 8, 2008.

187. Taylor, pp. 30, 46.

188. Robertson.

189. Rotberg, p. 109.

190. Naidu.

191 . Thembi Mutch, "China in East Africa: Win-Win?," Think Africa Press, May 8, 2012.

192. Brautigam,"The Dragon's Gift."

193. Shinn, "The Role of China in Africa."

194. Zhao.

195. "Sudan's Parliament Authorizes Confiscation of Oil Exports," *Sudan Tribune*, December 9, 2011.

196. "Chinese envoy urges peaceful settlement of Sudans dispute," *Sudan Tribune*, May 13, 2012.

197. As quoted in Alessi.

198. Morrison.

199. Stephen Burgess, "Sustainability of Strategic Minerals in Southern Africa and Potential Conflicts and Partnerships," Montgomery, AL: U.S. Air War College, 2011, draft.

200. Pham, March 29, 2012, p. 2.

201. Barney Jopson, "South Africa to China: Let's Make It About More Than Minerals," *Financial Times*, August 24, 2010.

202. Burgess.

203. *Ibid*.

204. Duncan Freeman, Jonathan Hoislag, and Steffi Weil, "China's Foreign Farming Policy," Brussels, Belgium: Brussels Institute of Contemporary China Studies, BICCS Asia Paper, Vol. 3, No. 9.

205. RSIS, "China's Food Security: Questioning the Numbers — Analysis," May 9, 2011, available from *www.eurasiareview.com*.

206. Simon Freemantle and Jeremy Stevens, "Insight and Strategy — China's Food Security Challenge: What Role for Africa?" Chicago, IL: Standard Bank, November 18, 2011.

207. "Lions on the Move."

208. "White Paper on China-Africa Economic and Trade Cooperation," People's Republic of China (PRC) Information Office of the State Council, December 1, 2010.

209. Brautigam and Tang, "China's Investment in African Special Economic Zones."

210. Brautigam, "The Dragon's Gift," pp. 236, 247.

211. "West Africa: The Downside of Foreign Land Acquisitions," IRIN News, January 19, 2012.

212. David Shinn, "Assessing China's Role and Influence in Africa," testimony before U.S. House of Representatives Subcommittee on Africa, Global Health, and Human Rights, March 29, 2012.

213. Poindexter Sama, "Agric Ministry Receives $1.2 Billion Investment for Rice and Rubber Production.," January 20, 2012, available from *www.farmlandgrab.org*.

214. Deborah Brautigam and Tang Xiaoyang, "China's Engagement in African Agriculture: Down to the Countryside," *The China Quarterly*, 2009.

215. Joachim von Braun and Ruth Meinzen-Dick, "'Land Grabbing' by Foreign Investors in Developing Countries: Risks and Opportunities," International Food Policy Research Institute, Policy Brief 13, April 2009.

216. Yongjun Zhao, "Engaging China on Africa's Agriculture," *The Newsletter*, No. 57, Summer 2011.

217. Rotberg, p. 15.

218. Shinn, "China's Growing Role in Africa."

219. Alden, pp. 35, 105.

220. "Inauguration of New AU Headquarters Celebrates China's Rise in Africa," January 28, 2012, available from *VOANews.com*.

221. PRC Premier Wen Jiabao, "Speech: Building the New Type of China-Africa Strategic Partnership," *Pambazuka News*, November 12, 2009.

222. Trilateral, p. 2.

223. David H. Shinn, "The United States and China in Africa: Advancing the Diplomatic Agenda," *Journal of Foreign Relations*, November 14, 2011.

224. Merle Kellerhais, Jr., "U.S. Diplomat Discusses Africa with Asian Counterparts," IIP Digital, Washington, DC: U.S. Department of State, November 22, 2011.

225. Swan, 2008.

226. Shinn, "China's Growing Role in Africa."

227. Yamamoto, March 29, 2012.

228. Wonacott.

229. "China Urges International Community to Assist in Fighting Piracy in Gulf of Guinea," *Xinhua*, October 19, 2011.

230. "Letter dated 18 January 2012 from the Secretary-General addressed to the President of the Security Council," New York: United Nations Security Council, S/2012/45.